JOHN D. ROCKEFELLER
ROBBER BARON
OR INDUSTRIAL STATESMAN?

Problems in American Civilization

UNDER THE EDITORIAL DIRECTION OF

George Rogers Taylor

John D. Rockefeller

ROBBER BARON

OR INDUSTRIAL STATESMAN?

EDITED WITH AN INTRODUCTION BY

Earl Latham

Problems in American Civilization

READINGS SELECTED BY THE
DEPARTMENT OF AMERICAN STUDIES
AMHERST COLLEGE

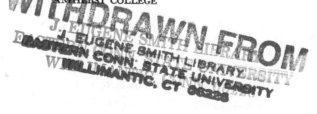
D. C. HEATH AND COMPANY: Boston

CT
275
.R75
L3

INTRODUCTION

THE businessman is a symbol of American culture the world around, and for many people that symbol was personified by John D. Rockefeller. No other time or place has produced his like. The architect of the first great American trust, Rockefeller was attacked and defended with violent passion by the struggling partisans of industrialism and of social reform in the years after the Civil War. Long before his death he had become a semilegendary character who appeared to the general public either as a demon of avarice and extortion, crushing without scruple those who stood in his way, or as a high-minded philanthropist, bestowing his bounty with charitable devotion to good works. The first selection here reprinted, an excerpt from John T. Flynn's *God's Gold*, introduces Rockefeller in his dual role of a man loathed and loved and throws light upon his personal reaction to the attacks made upon him.

A representative leader of the powerful group of businessmen who made their appearance with the revolution in industry after the Civil War, Rockefeller was singled out by critics of the emerging social order because of the spectacular way in which he created his oil empire. During the administrations of Theodore Roosevelt there appeared in print a series of attacks upon corruption in industry and politics. To their authors — among whom Ida M. Tarbell was one of the first, and indeed one of the most painstaking

and responsible — Roosevelt gave the opprobrious name "muckrakers," after the Man with the Muckrake in *Pilgrim's Progress*, who was more preoccupied with filth than with future bliss. In her monumental investigation of *The History of the Standard Oil Company*, however, Miss Tarbell seemed more impressed by another text of Bunyan's, *The Life and Death of Mr. Badman*, which says of extortion that it is "most commonly committed by men of trade, who without all conscience, when they have an advantage, will make a prey of their neighbor." The readings present a long excerpt from Miss Tarbell's account of the methods by which the Standard Oil monopoly of her day was created and the manner in which it functioned.

Miss Tarbell's strictures are made largely from the point of view of personal ethics. Those expressed by Matthew Josephson in the selection from his book *The Robber Barons* show more specific concern with social and political values. Josephson is a critic of monopoly capitalism, and his account of the development of Standard Oil reflects his opinion that profits are the principal goal of enterprise and that technological progress and social service are only accidental by-products. Not at all surprisingly, a contrary judgment is expressed by Rockefeller himself in the next selection, a chapter from his *Random Reminiscences of Men and Events*. Here the motivation of profits is represented as secondary to

Rockefeller's ambition to create order, economy, and efficiency in the oil industry.

Of particular interest to students of social and economic institutions is the way in which railroad rebates and other forms of discrimination were employed by Rockefeller in building the oil monopoly. Although it seems clear that Standard Oil did not invent the rebate, it is equally clear that it was utilized by Rockefeller and his associates in ingenious and artful ways to kill competition, and even to dominate the railroads themselves. The first selection below from Allan Nevins's *John D. Rockefeller* ("Rebates and Standard Oil") discusses the uses to which railroad rebates were put. Such rebates were not illegal in the earliest days of railroad development, but it was largely the widespread feeling that this form of discrimination had been abused by the railroads in favor of Rockefeller which led the states and the federal government to declare them unlawful.

A just evaluation of Rockefeller cannot be separated from an appraisal of the early political and social conditions under which industrial enterprise first flourished. This in turn raises serious questions about the relation which ought to exist between private enterprise and government — questions which are among the most pressing issues of contemporary public policy. At what point does it become desirable for government to intervene in the workings of the industrial system to protect those who are not capable of surviving without such intervention? How can government conciliate the rival claims of liberty for those who prosper and security for those who don't? Is free competition an effective regulator of the public interest in a natural resource industry? If order and efficiency are to be imposed upon an industry in which competition wastes important natural resources, what is the case for private regulation of the industry by its principal members, in the manner of Rockefeller and his associates? What is the case for public regulation? What are the elements of desirable public policy towards industrial giantism? What should be the respective roles of government and private enterprise in the development of new forms of industrial activity? An appraisal of Rockefeller will depend in part upon one's choices about public policy in the relation of government to private enterprise, and contrariwise, Rockefeller's career will help to inform these choices.

It was with Standard Oil and Rockefeller in mind that Henry Demarest Lloyd put questions like these six and seven decades ago. Lloyd anticipated the "muckrakers" by twenty years when he first attacked Standard Oil in 1880 in the *Atlantic Monthly*. He regarded "trusts" with strong disfavor and in 1894 stated his antipathy in what, in its time, was a powerful book, *Wealth against Commonwealth*, written in vivid style with evangelical vigor. Chapter 34 of this work, titled "The Old Self-Interest," is placed next in the readings as a sample of Lloyd's appraisal of the system of which Standard Oil was a part.

In 1902, Gilbert H. Montague wrote, "In a matter so much discussed as . . . [the Standard Oil Company] there seems no longer room for unverified opinion." The need for informed judgments and verified opinions is perhaps even greater now, when the free enterprise system itself, although vigorous and productive in the United States, has been abandoned in other parts of the globe. But there are still difficulties in the way of reaching such judgments and opinions, as the last four selections illustrate. All of these represent a single controversy over the

validation of certain facts about Rockefeller and Standard Oil, and over the
proper evaluation to be made of Rockefeller in the light of these and other facts.

The center of this controversy is really
Henry Demarest Lloyd, and the argument is whether Lloyd made a fair appraisal of Rockefeller and Standard Oil
on the basis of accurate facts. The second
selection from Nevins's life of Rockefeller
("A General Evaluation") strikes a balance of judgment that favors Rockefeller
and revises downward an earlier favorable estimate of Lloyd's conclusions.
Lewis Galantière in "John D.: An Academy Portrait" finds the Nevins appraisal
lacking in important respects, and Chester McA. Destler in "Wealth against
Commonwealth, 1894 and 1944" seeks to
restore and support the earlier judgment
made by Lloyd. Destler is answered by
Nevins in "Letter to the Editor of the
American Historical Review," which re-
asserts his charges against Lloyd's accuracy and objectivity. What appears to
be merely a dispute among craftsmen
about technique is really a fundamental
conflict over interpretation of a significant economic phenomenon. All of these
writers indicate preferences and make
choices as to what they believe to be
"good" and "bad." The reader will feel
free to do the same.

Rockefeller's career focuses several
aspects of modern American culture and
raises numerous questions which appear
from time to time in the form of public
issues. One of these involves the problem
of how wealth is accumulated. Must it
come by exploitation, as Jefferson and
John Taylor of Caroline thought it did?
Or is it to be regarded as the natural
reward of patience, frugality, and virtue,
as the Right Reverend William Lawrence
of Boston conceived it? Does the record

of Rockefeller contribute anything to a
settlement of this persistent controversy?

A related issue is whether bigness in
industry is the result of conspiracy or of
inevitable and irresistible pressures from
blind forces operating unmindful of the
will of man. Lloyd thought that it was
the first. William Graham Sumner of
Yale thought that something like evolution in biology operated also in social
relations, and that integration was the
natural and inevitable result of this process. Do the life of Rockefeller and the
history of the Standard Oil trust provide
any material that is helpful in appraising
these conflicting views?

Again, what is the role of the business
leader or entrepreneur in the country's
economic development? How are we to
assess his contribution to this development in matters of production and in
matters of finance? Thorstein Veblen
considered the entrepreneur to be less
important in the development of modern
industry than the engineer and the
worker. Modern studies in the administration of private and public enterprises
tend to augment and enhance the function, and therefore the importance, of the
executive or manager of large and complicated undertakings. To what extent
will Rockefeller's career support or refute
Veblen's thesis?

A fourth but by no means final question is the nature of the responsibility of
the man of wealth and power for the
administration of his wealth and power.
Is it his to possess and administer as he
chooses, or has he a public trust to dis-
charge? If the latter, what is the nature
of this trust and responsibility? How, if
it exists, should it be enforced? This
problem, like the preceding ones, is
illuminated by a study of Rockefeller's
career.

CONTENTS

THE CLASH OF ISSUES

His accusers rhetorically asked:

"Shall we buy cheap of Captain Kidd, and shut our ears to the agony that rustles in his silks?"

— HENRY DEMAREST LLOYD

Others disagreed:

"He was a bold innovator in both industry and philanthropy; . . . he brought to the first a great unifying idea, which he insisted should be thoroughly tested, and to the second a stronger, more expert, and more enduring type of organization."

— ALLAN NEVINS

Many believed him to be great:

"If to live in advance of one's time, to be the first on the ground in the direction of progress, is greatness, John D. Rockefeller is great."

— MARCUS M. BROWN

Others observed:

"But his mouth was a slit, like a shark's."

— MATTHEW JOSEPHSON

To account for his fabulous fortune, one writer declared:

"America is the habitat of the self-made man, and the self-made man is a pecuniary organism."

— THORSTEIN VEBLEN

But Rockefeller simply said:

"God gave me my money."

John T. Flynn: THE MUCKRAKERS

IN April, 1906, while fighting to put through his railroad bill, Roosevelt in a speech dedicating the new House of Representatives Office Building, made a reference to the Man with the Muckrake in Bunyan's "Pilgrim's Progress," "the man who could look no way but downward with the muckrake in his hand," who could not see the celestial crown offered him because he continued to "rake to himself the filth of the floor." He was repeating a phrase which he had used a few weeks before at the gridiron dinner.

Roosevelt was referring to that extraordinary group of journalists who, in magazines and books and newspapers, were uncovering the amazing graft of business and politics and were producing what the *Atlantic Monthly* called the "literature of exposure." This eruption of denunciatory writing constituted a phenomenon in the life of the time and exercised a powerful effect upon the public mind. As in all movements, the dramatic narratives of dishonesty in high places came from the pens of a mixture of serious and able men and from pure sensation mongers. Roosevelt's unlucky phrase grouped them all together and furnished his own enemies with an odious label which they proceeded to make powerful use of. Every critic thereafter was called a muckraker. Every unfriendly discussion of the vast, undisciplined pestilence of knavery in big business and public life

was refuted by being branded as muckraking. No historian of the times now pretends to deny not merely that grave abuses grew up, but that the public conscience seemed to have become inert. That the revelations of the so-called muckrakers, which turned the light upon these dark places, were the most potent agent in awakening that languid conscience, cannot be denied. Roosevelt's phrase did an injustice to the earnest writers and editors who not only furnished for him the most effective support he got but made a contribution of lasting benefit to the developments of the time. . . .

The movement had been gathering strength for some time. Its beginnings must be traced to about 1894 when Henry Demarest Lloyd published his "Wealth against Commonwealth." Lloyd might perhaps be called the Father of the Muckrakers. After that the next impetus came from the newspapers. Joseph Pulitzer and William Randolph Hearst were publishing in almost savage rivalry the *World* and the *Journal*. Both put themselves on the side of what came to be referred to with varying affection or scorn as the "masses." Exposures of corrupt politicians, franchise-grabbing traction magnates, ice trust managers, "malefactors" of all sorts filled the pages of these papers, which the more conservative publishers referred to as "yellow journals." For some years a magazine known as the *Arena*, ably edited, took the popular side and monthly produced articles of exposure of various political and economic abuses. In 1902 there began to appear in *McClure's Magazine* a "History of Standard Oil," by Ida M. Tarbell.[1] Ida M. Tarbell had already made a considerable impression with a "Life of Lincoln" which was printed serially in *McClure's* and increased the circulation of that magazine in an amazing way. She was a woman of exceptional ability as an editor and writer who had had a special training at the Sorbonne in Paris in the technique of historical research. She was born in the oil regions, grew up there, as a child had heard the incessant discussion and agitation following the great battles between the producers and Rockefeller. Her family had been engaged in the oil industry and her brother was at this time an official of the Pure Oil Company, the indomitable independent group which alone had been able to successfully hold its place against the Standard. . . .

Miss Tarbell spent two years following the course of Rockefeller's company, visiting the oil regions, Rockefeller's early homes in New York, Cleveland, and other oil centers. And in 1902 *McClure's Magazine* began publication of her story. The serial ran for two years and was read with hungry interest by people everywhere. Miss Tarbell retold again much of the early history and many of the incidents which had been

first narrated by Lloyd. But she had the benefit of a fuller understanding of those events and the accumulation of a great mass of data which were not open to Lloyd. Besides she carried the story further along — to the formation of the Pure Oil Company in the late nineties. She talked with Lloyd at the outset of her labors and while her story was being published Lloyd followed it and expressed the greatest satisfaction and delight at her fine performance.

Miss Tarbell's story was not, of course, a life of Rockefeller, but a record of the abuses of the Standard Oil Company from 1872 to 1898. It was a mixture of historical narrative and indictment. No critic could complain that she had not examined the facts, for the evidences of minute and painstaking investigation were stamped upon every part of the work. Less dramatic in its style than Lloyd's book, it was nevertheless far more dramatic through the skillful management of its incidents. An analysis of a great economic episode pushed forward serially through two years (later in two volumes) with remorseless logic, it was at the same time a story of absorbing interest. Of this remarkable book it is just to say that it remains to this day the ablest document of its kind ever produced by an American writer.

The success of this monumental work was so great that before it had been completely published as a serial critics of the current vogue of graft in business and politics sprang up everywhere and the age of the muckrakers was in full career. Burton J. Kendrick told the story of the Astor Fortune and writers like David Graham Phillips with his "Treason of the Senate," Lincoln Steffens with his "Shame of the Cities," and dozens of others dealt crippling blows at the respectability of some of our commercial

[1] Lincoln Steffens in his Autobiography (Harcourt, Brace and Company, 1931) assigns to his article in *McClure's Magazine*, October, 1902, the honor of being the "first muckraking article." It was called "Tweed Days in St. Louis" and told of Joseph W. Folk's battle against the St. Louis boodlers. However, when Steffens went to *McClure's*, Ida Tarbell had already begun work on her history of Standard Oil. And long before Steffens' articles magazines like the *Arena* had been pressing the work for exposure.

and political nobility. The movement for Pure Food laws, for honesty in advertising and against the patent medicine fakirs which got its impetus from Dr. Harvey Wiley and his "Poison Squad" in the Department of Agriculture was pushed with dramatic fervor by magazines like *Collier's*. Thomas W. Lawson electrified the country for a while with his "Frenzied Finance," published as a serial in *Everybody's*. This was a lurid, highly fevered account of the operations of Henry H. Rogers and William Rockefeller and James Stillman in Amalgamated Copper, Boston Gas, and other hectic financial stock manipulations. The whole subject of the grasping, unscrupulous, domineering business man and his corrupt political ally got into fiction and on the stage. And by a kind of fatality each offense fastened on other rich men and each blast of invective hurled at others, left another coating of infamy upon the name of Rockefeller. "There are worse men than John D. Rockefeller," said the *Arena*. "There is probably not one, however, who in the public mind so typifies the grave and startling menace to the social order." He had indeed taken on the character of a symbol. He was the victim of another circumstance. The same writer expressed it. "John D. has one vulnerable point, his religious instinct. Dissimulator and hypocrite by nature, the so-called development of veneration is nevertheless plainly marked." People felt less repugnance for the heretical Carnegie or the unregenerate John W. Gates or the worldly Rogers or the magnificent Morgan than they did for the pious John D. who was put down as a hypocrite, giving with one hand to countless charities and with the other collecting back the sum of his bounty from the poor by raising the price of kerosene.

As in the case of Lloyd, so Rockefeller kept his peace in the face of the Tarbell articles. In the South a friend undertook to suggest that he would reply on some points to Miss Tarbell. "Not a word!" Rockefeller interrupted. "Not a word about that misguided woman." Gaylord Wilshire met Rockefeller at a banquet in Santa Barbara and asked him about the Tarbell articles. "All without foundation," Rockefeller replied. "The idea of the Standard forcing any one to sell his refinery is absurd. The refiners wanted to sell to us and nobody that has sold and worked with us but has made money and is glad he did so. I thought once of having an answer made to the *McClure* articles, but you know it has always been the policy of the Standard to keep silent under attack and let our acts speak for themselves."

The orgy of denunciation and exposure got a lively and sensational turn from an attack on Rockefeller from within the church which loaded his name with more odium and gave him more pain perhaps than any other which he suffered. In April, 1905, he gave very secretly $100,000 to the American Board of Commissioners of Foreign Missions, a Congregational body. A body of Congregational ministers meeting in Boston engaged in a hectic debate over a resolution that "the acceptance of such a gift involves the constituents of the board in a relation implying honor to the donor and subjects the board to the charge of ignoring . . . the repeated and formidable indictments in specific terms for methods which are morally iniquitous and socially destructive." Immediately the newspapers broke out into a violent discussion of "tainted money," a phrase which was to share with "muckrakers" the popularity of the papers for some years. Every editor, educator, and preacher in the country contributed his view to the propriety of accepting Rockefeller's money. Precious few said a word for Rockefeller himself. There were many, however, who, while condemning the manner in which Rockefeller made his money, defended the gift. Of course, the clerical and pedagogical beneficiaries of his gifts came bravely to his defense. "Why let the devil have all the good tunes?" said the New York *World*. Letters poured in to the New York *Tribune* which made much of the matter. One of these urged that the money "be taken out of its evil path," and used the phrase "the tainted money of Judas," from which, perhaps, the term "tainted money" sprang. "Take it from the unspeakable Turk; take it from the devil himself. Above all take it from a bad man, a gambler, a thief, if with his wickedness he has a weakness for doing good. Let the taint in some of his money be cleansed. Let the gold as well as the wroth of a bad man prove the good," suggested the *Independent*.

The Memphis *Commercial Appeal* expressed most graphically the essence of the attacks. "Captain Kidd was a pirate. If he had quietly dropped into a New England town some night and left a lot of stolen goods with a fence he would be liable under the law. If on the other hand he had made his way to a parsonage, told the minister who he was and that he wanted to make a present of 10,000 Spanish doubloons to build a new chapel, what would be thought of the preacher who could accept that which it would be a crime for a fence to receive?"

The most redoubtable of all Rockefeller's assailants was the Rev. Washington Gladden, of Ohio, a widely known preacher of the day and a moderator of the Congregational Church. Gladden indeed moved merrily to the attack. Gladden was a product of the Finger Lake Region, like Rockefeller, and actually went to the old Owego Academy where Rockefeller got his early education. He had been belaboring Rockefeller for many years. Now he raked over Rockefeller's past to prove the charge of the Boston ministers that Rockefeller's money had been obtained by "methods morally iniquitous and socially destructive." He filed a written protest with the Prudential Committee of the Congregational Church. "The good that is done," he protested, "by lowering our ethical standards might best be left undone. Shall the young men and women of the missionary colleges be taught to regard Mr. Rockefeller as a great benefactor? The colleges might better be closed."

At first the Prudential Committee declared the gift had come "voluntarily and unsolicited," giving an impression that to refuse it would be an ungracious and unChristian act. They spoke of it as a "surprise." They maintained this attitude until Frederick T. Gates threatened to expose their importunities if they did not reveal frankly the conditions under which Rockefeller made the gift. As a matter of fact, the gift had been made reluctantly by Rockefeller only after he had been pestered by the Rev. James Barton, of the Committee. Both young John D. and Frederick T. Gates had written Barton refusing the interviews he asked with the old man. But Barton kept up his importunities and finally Gates sent $100,000 saying very significantly, "There is no reason known to me on Mr. Rockefeller's part why you should make any distinction in acknowledging this contribution than if it had been made by any one else."

The religious journals flew to Rockefeller's defense, approved the gift and the man who made it. Dr. Lyman Abbott in the *Outlook* thought the Boston protest showed the church could not be bought. Certainly it proved no such thing for the church officials approved and accepted the gift. Those who denounced it were rebels in a small minority.

Rockefeller himself, throughout, though deeply pained and chagrined, remained silent. He went to prayer meeting at Euclid Avenue Baptist Church where he was received with acclaim and asked to speak. He talked a little and then said: "I have talked too long, I am afraid. There are others here who want to talk. I don't want you to think I am a selfish monopolist." The congregation caught the meaning and laughed and applauded him heartily.

Gladden told reporters he was going to start a movement against accepting gifts from rich malefactors but the agitation soon died down. The appetite for gifts from "those rich malefactors" was too extensive and voracious. In the midst of it all Rockefeller made his contribution of $10,000,000 to the General Education Board. The agitation undoubtedly left a deep stain upon his name, but it made some friends for Rockefeller too. "What was intended," said *Current History*, "as an earnest, intelligent protest, took on the character of an uproar, made Rockefeller look like a much abused man and brought him much undeserved sympathy."

The unreasoning distinction made against Rockefeller among rich men was a little puzzling. The same papers which fulminated against the oil man, supported the countless local pleas being made everywhere to Andrew Carnegie for libraries. A candid, unbiased examination of the Rockefeller fortune at this time must have forced any man to admit that of all our great fortunes it was the most honestly acquired. Rockefeller had dealt honestly with his associates, with his workmen, and with his customers. His wealth had been accumulated out of the profits of building a great industrial enterprise. His offenses had been committed almost wholly against his competitors. They consisted in those deceptions, intrigues, and stratagems which had always been employed in business against rivals. They seemed worse perhaps because used upon a larger field. Also they got so much advertisement. But they were employed not as the main engine of his success, but merely as part of a larger design; they were incidents in a grandiose scheme of industrial empire building which had as its fundamental, major objective the development and perfection of a new system of business — a system which was destined very soon to be universally adopted. The cruelty of Rockefeller's own conduct is much magnified by focusing the attention upon the sufferings of the victim, particularly when we overlook altogether the part which stupidity and ignorance of most of the victims played in their own destruction. For years the Rockefeller legend was the story of little men crushed. The tale of a small refiner or dealer brought to ruin always made an appealing story. The constructive work of Rockefeller in building a great business and in pioneering in the field of efficiency and honest administration within the business itself was wholly overlooked. Even the establishment at this time of a pension system for old employees, thirty years in advance of scores of large business concerns today, was almost completely passed over. The distinction between the Rockefeller fortune made by way of accumulated profit in the building not merely of a great business but a great business system and those fortunes made by the group of glorified stock-jobbers like Morgan and Gates and Havemeyer and Moore and Reid and Gould and others was utterly overlooked. You will look in vain in the Standard Oil Company for performances like the organization of United States Steel where plants were bought for double and treble their value in stock and where promoters' fees running to hundreds of millions of dollars were drawn out by the organizers and where the entire half-billion shares of common stock had no physical property whatever back of it. The Standard Oil was never over-capitalized. Indeed, it was always under-capitalized. When Rockefeller acquired a company he paid its actual value in cash or stock. There was no water. And this, oddly, was one of the first causes of his damnation. It came from the sellers who thought they ought to get fancy prices for the "good will" of their business. And even so intelligent a critic as Ida Tarbell joined in this reproof without, it seems, quite understanding its import.

All this was very puzzling to Rockefeller. "Standard Oil," he said later, "has no water in its stock, has never issued bonds or shares through bankers, no underwriting syndicates of selling schemes, has always paid bills, keeps 60,000 men employed, pays well, cares for them when sick, pensions them when old, brought a million dollars a week into the country."

Yet he was loaded with contumely and shame while the Morgans and Carnegies and Garys and others were honored. Carnegie had sold armor plate to the Russians for $249 and exacted from the United States Navy from $520 to $700 a ton. Moreover a congressional committee had said of the steel leaders, Carnegie, Corey, Schwab, "The unblushing character of the frauds to which these men have been parties and the disregard for truth and honesty which they have shown for our committee render them unworthy of credence."

Out of the capitalizations of Morgan countless millions of dollars had been lost by the hapless thousands of investors who had been lured into putting their savings into the outrageously watered stocks. When the panic of 1907 came all the industrialists in steel and copper and cotton cut wages, but Standard Oil not only did not cut wages but increased employment by providing during the recession for extensive construction works, an expedient for depressions which today, more than twenty years later, we are still considering.

Rockefeller could not, therefore, understand what could be the explanation of the odium in which he was held while his fellow capitalists came in merely for a kind of good-natured spoofing, from the people who otherwise admired them.

As for his money and his gifts, he said nothing, though he was stung into submitting to his first interview. This was in the *Woman's Home Companion* in 1915. And in that he made merely an indirect reference to the storm which raged around his gifts. He said: "God gave me my money."

Ida M. Tarbell:

THE STANDARD OIL COMPANY

THE strides the firm of Rockefeller and Andrews made after the former went into it were attributed for three or four years mainly to his extraordinary capacity for bargaining and borrowing. Then its chief competitors began to suspect something. John Rockefeller might get his oil cheaper now and then, they said, but he could not do it often. He might make close contracts for which they had neither the patience nor the stomach. He might have an unusual mechanical and practical genius in his partner. But these things could not explain all. They believed they bought, on the whole, almost as cheaply as he, and they knew they made as good oil and with as great, or nearly as great, economy. He could sell at no better price than they. Where was his advantage? There was but one place where it could be, and that was in transportation. He must be getting better rates from the railroads than they were. In 1868 or 1869 a member of a rival firm long in the business, which had been prosperous from the start, and which prided itself on its methods, its economy and its energy, Alexander, Scofield and Company, went to the Atlantic and Great Western road, then under the Erie management, and complained. "You are giving others better rates than you are us," said Mr. Alexander, the representative of the firm. "We cannot compete if

you do that." The railroad agent did not attempt to deny it — he simply agreed to give Mr. Alexander a rebate also. The arrangement was interesting. Mr. Alexander was to pay the open, or regular, rate on oil from the Oil Regions to Cleveland, which was then forty cents a barrel. At the end of each month he was to send to the railroad vouchers for the amount of oil shipped and paid for at forty cents, and was to get back from the railroad, in money, fifteen cents on each barrel. This concession applied only to oil brought from the wells. He was never able to get a rebate on oil shipped eastward.[1] According to Mr. Alexander, the Atlantic and Great Western gave the rebates on oil from the Oil Regions to Cleveland up to 1871 and the system was then discontinued. Late in 1871, however, the firm for the first time got a rebate on the Lake Shore road on oil brought from the field.

Another Cleveland man, W. H. Doane, engaged in shipping crude oil, began to suspect about the same time as Mr. Alexander that the Standard was receiving rebates. Now Mr. Doane had always been opposed to the "drawback business," but it was impossible for him to supply his customers with crude oil at as low a rate as the Standard paid if it received a rebate

1 Testimony of Mr. Alexander before the Committee of Commerce of the United States House of Representatives, April, 1872.

and he did not, and when it was first generally rumoured in Cleveland that the railroads were favouring Mr. Rockefeller he went to see the agent of the road. "I told him I did not want any drawback, unless others were getting it; I wanted it if they were getting it, and he gave me at that time ten cents drawback." This arrangement Mr. Doane said had lasted but a short time. At the date he was speaking — the spring of 1872 — he had had no drawback for two years.

A still more important bit of testimony as to the time when rebates first began to be given to the Cleveland refiners and as to who first got them and why, is contained in an affidavit made in 1880 by the very man who made the discrimination.[2] This man was General J. H. Devereux, who in 1868 succeeded Amasa Stone as vice-president of the Lake Shore Railroad. General Devereux said that his experience with the oil traffic had begun with his connection with the Lake Shore; that the only written memorandum concerning oil which he found in his office on entering his new position was a book in which it was stated that the representatives of the twenty-five oil-refining firms in Cleveland had agreed to pay a cent a gallon on crude oil removed from the Oil Regions. General Devereux says that he soon found there was a deal of trouble in store for him over oil freight. The competition between the twenty-five firms was close, the Pennsylvania was "claiming a patent right" on the transportation of oil and was putting forth every effort to make Pittsburgh and Philadelphia the chief refining centres. Oil Creek was boasting that it was going to be the future refining point for the world. All of this looked bad for what General Devereux speaks of as

the "then very limited refining capacity of Cleveland." This remark shows how new he was to the business, for, as we have already seen, Cleveland in 1868 had anything but a limited refining capacity. Between three and four million dollars were invested in oil refineries, and the town was receiving within 35,000 barrels of as much oil as New York City, and within 300,000 as much as Pittsburgh, and it was boasting that the next year it would outstrip these competitors, which, as a matter of fact, it did.

The natural point for General Devereux to consider, of course, was whether he could meet the rates the Pennsylvania were giving and increase the oil freight for the Lake Shore. The road had a branch running to Franklin, Pennsylvania, within a few miles of Oil City. This he completed, and then, as he says in his affidavit, "a sharper contest than ever was produced growing out of the opposition of the Pennsylvania Railroad in competition. Such rates and arrangements were made by the Pennsylvania Railroad that it was publicly proclaimed in the public print in Oil City, Titusville and other places that Cleveland was to be wiped out as a refining centre as with a sponge." General Devereux goes on to say that all the refiners of the town, without exception, came to him in alarm, and expressed their fears that they would have either to abandon their business there or move to Titusville or other points in the Oil Regions; that the only exception to this decision was that offered by Rockefeller, Andrews and Flagler, who, on his assurance that the Lake Shore Railroad could and would handle oil as cheaply as the Pennsylvania Company, proposed to stand their ground at Cleveland and fight it out on that line. And so General Devereux gave the Standard the rebate on the rate which Amasa Stone had made

[2] . . . At the time General Devereux made this affidavit, 1880, he was president of the New York, Pennsylvania and Ohio Railroad.

with all the refiners. Why he should not have quieted the fears of the twenty-four or twenty-five other refiners by lowering their rate, too, does not appear in the affidavit. At all events the rebate had come, and, as we have seen, it soon was suspected and others went after it, and in some cases got it. But the rebate seems to have been granted generally only on oil brought from the Oil Regions. Mr. Alexander claims he was never able to get his rate lowered on his Eastern shipments. The railroad took the position with him that if he could ship as much oil as the Standard he could have as low a rate, but not otherwise. Now in 1870 the Standard Oil Company had a daily capacity of about 1,500 barrels of crude. The refinery was the largest in the town, though it had some close competitors. Nevertheless on the strength of its large capacity it received the special favour. It was a plausible way to get around the theory generally held then, as now, though not so definitely crystallised into law, that the railroad being a common carrier had no right to discriminate between its patrons. It remained to be seen whether the practice would be accepted by Mr. Rockefeller's competitors without a contest, or, if contested, would be supported by the law.

What the Standard's rebate on Eastern shipments was in 1870 it is impossible to say. Mr. Alexander says he was never able to get a rate lower than $1.33 a barrel by rail, and that it was commonly believed in Cleveland that the Standard had a rate of ninety cents. Mr. Flagler, however, the only member of the firm who has been examined under oath on that point, showed, by presenting the contract of the Standard Oil Company with the Lake Shore road in 1870, that the rates varied during the year from $1.40 to $1.20 and $1.60, according to the season. When

Mr. Flagler was asked if there was no drawback or rebate on this rate he answered, "None whatever."

It would seem from the above as if the one man in the Cleveland oil trade in 1870 who ought to have been satisfied was Mr. Rockefeller. His was the largest firm in the largest refining centre of the country; that is, of the 10,000 to 12,000 daily capacity divided among the twenty-five or twenty-six refiners of Cleveland he controlled 1,500 barrels. Not only was Cleveland the largest refining centre in the country, it was gaining rapidly, for where in 1868 it shipped 776,356 barrels of refined oil, in 1869 it shipped 923,933, in 1870 1,459,500, and in 1871 1,640,499.[3] Not only did Mr. Rockefeller control the largest firm in this most prosperous centre of a prosperous business, he controlled one of amazing efficiency. The combination, in 1870, of the various companies with which he was connected had brought together a group of remarkable men. Samuel Andrews, by all accounts, was the ablest mechanical superintendent in Cleveland. William Rockefeller, the brother of John D. Rockefeller, was not only an energetic and intelligent business man, he was a man whom people liked. He was open-hearted, jolly, a good story-teller, a man who knew and liked a good horse — not too pious, as some of John's business associates thought him, not a man to suspect or fear, as many a man did John. Old oil men will tell you on the creek today how much they liked him in the days when he used to come to Oil City buying oil for the Cleveland firm. The personal quality of William Rockefeller was, and always has been, a strong asset of the Standard Oil Company. Probably the strongest man in the firm after John D. Rockefeller was Henry M.

[3] Report for 1871 of the Cleveland Board of Trade.

Flagler. He was like the others, a young man, and one who, like the head of the firm, had the passion for money, and in a hard self-supporting experience, begun when but a boy, had learned, as well as his chief, some of the principles of making it. He was untiring in his efforts to increase the business, quick to see an advantage, as quick to take it. He had no scruples to make him hesitate over the ethical quality of a contract which was advantageous. Success, that is, making money, was its own justification. He was not a secretive man, like John D. Rockefeller, not a dreamer, but he could keep his mouth shut when necessary and he knew the worth of a financial dream when it was laid before him. It must have been evident to every business man who came in contact with the young Standard Oil Company that it would go far. The firm itself must have known it would go far. Indeed nothing could have stopped the Standard Oil Company in 1870 — the oil business being what it was — but an entire change in the nature of the members of the firm, and they were not the kind of material which changes.

With such a set of associates, with his organisation complete from his buyers on the creek to his exporting agent in New York, with the transportation advantages which none of his competitors had had the daring or the persuasive power to get, certainly Mr. Rockefeller should have been satisfied in 1870. But Mr. Rockefeller was far from satisfied. He was a brooding, cautious, secretive man, seeing all the possible dangers as well as all the possible opportunities in things, and he studied, as a player at chess, all the possible combinations which might imperil his supremacy. These twenty-five Cleveland rivals of his — how could he at once and forever put them out of the game? He and his part-

ners had somehow conceived a great idea — the advantages of combination. What might they not do if they could buy out and absorb the big refineries now competing with them in Cleveland? The possibilities of the idea grew as they discussed it. Finally they began tentatively to sound some of their rivals. But there were other rivals than these at home. There were the creek refiners! They were there at the mouth of the wells. What might not this geographical advantage do in time? Refining was going on there on an increasing scale; the capacity of the Oil Regions had indeed risen to nearly 10,000 barrels a day — equal to that of New York, exceeding that of Pittsburgh by nearly 4,000 barrels, and almost equalling that of Cleveland. The men of the oil country loudly declared that they meant to refine for the world. They boasted of an oil kingdom which eventually should handle the entire business and compel Cleveland and Pittsburgh either to abandon their works or bring them to the oil country. In this boastful ambition they were encouraged particularly by the Pennsylvania Railroad, which naturally handled the largest percentage of the oil. How long could the Standard Oil Company stand against this competition?

There was another interest as deeply concerned as Mr. Rockefeller in preserving Cleveland's supremacy as a refining centre, and this was the Lake Shore and New York Central Railroads. Let the bulk of refining be done in the Oil Regions and these roads were in danger of losing a profitable branch of business. This situation in regard to the oil traffic was really more serious now than in 1868 when General Devereux had first given the Standard a rebate. Then it was that the Pennsylvania, through its lusty ally the Empire Transportation Company;

Tarbell · THE STANDARD OIL COMPANY   **11**

was making the chief fight to secure a "patent right on oil transportation." The Erie was now becoming as aggressive a competitor. Gould and Fisk had gone into the fight with the vigour and the utter unscrupulousness which characterised all their dealings. They were allying themselves with the Pennsylvania Transportation Company, the only large rival pipe-line system which the Empire had. They were putting up a refinery near Jersey City and they were taking advantage shrewdly of all the speculative features of the new business.

As competition grew between the roads, they grew more reckless in granting rebates, the refiners more insistent in demanding them. By 1871 things had come to such a pass in the business that every refiner suspected his neighbour to be getting better rates than he. The result was that the freight agents were constantly beset for rebates, and that the large shippers were generally getting them on the ground of the quantity of oil they controlled. Indeed it was evident that the rebate being admitted, the only way in which it could be adjusted with a show of fairness was to grade it according to the size of the shipment.

Under these conditions of competition it was certain that the New York Central system must work if it was to keep its great oil freight, and the general freight agent of the Lake Shore road began to give the question special attention. This man was Peter H. Watson. Mr. Watson was an able patent lawyer who served under the strenuous Stanton as an Assistant-Secretary of War, and served well. After the war he had been made general freight agent of the Lake Shore and Michigan Southern Railroad, and later president of the branch of that road which ran into the Oil Regions. He had oil interests principally at Franklin, Pennsylvania, and was well known to all oil men. He was a business intimate of Mr. Rockefeller and a warm friend of Horace F. Clark, the son-in-law of W. H. Vanderbilt, at that time president of the Lake Shore and Michigan Southern Railroad. As the Standard Oil Company was the largest shipper in Cleveland and had already received the special favour from the Lake Shore which General Devereux describes, it was natural that Mr. Watson should consult frequently with Mr. Rockefeller on the question of holding and increasing his oil freight. It was equally natural, too, that Mr. Rockefeller should use his influence with Mr. Watson to strengthen the theory so important to his rapid growth — the theory that the biggest shipper should have the best rate.

Two other towns shared Cleveland's fear of the rise of the Oil Regions as a refining centre, and they were Pittsburgh and Philadelphia, and Mr. Rockefeller and Mr. Watson found in certain refiners of these places a strong sympathy with any plan which looked to holding the region in check. But while the menace in their geographical positions was the first ground of sympathy between these gentlemen, something more than local troubles occupied them. This was the condition of the refining business as a whole. It was unsatisfactory in many particulars. First, it was overdone. The great profits on refined oil and the growing demand for it had naturally caused a great number to rush into its manufacture. There was at this time a refining capacity of three barrels to every one produced. To be sure, few if any of these plants expected to run the year around. Then, as to-day, there were nearly always some stills in even the most prosperous works shut down. But after making a fair allowance for this fact there was still a much larger amount of refining actually done than the market demanded. The result was that the price of refined oil was steadily falling. Where Mr. Rockefeller had received on an average 58¾ cents a gallon for the oil he exported in 1865, the year he went into business, in 1870 he received but 26¾ cents. In 1865 he had a margin of forty-three cents, out of which to pay for transportation, manufacturing, barrelling and marketing and to make his profits. In 1870 he had but 17⅛ cents with which to do all this. To be sure his expenses had fallen enormously between 1865 and 1870, but so had his profits. The multiplication of refiners with the intense competition threatened to cut them down still lower. Naturally Mr. Rockefeller and his friends looked with dismay on this lowering of profits through gaining competition.

Another anxiety of the American refiners was the condition of the export trade. Oil had risen to fourth place in the exports of the United States in the twelve years since its discovery, and every year larger quantities were consumed abroad, but it was crude oil, not refined, which the foreigners were beginning to demand; that is, they had found they could import crude, refine it at home, and sell it cheaper than they could buy American refined. France, to encourage her home refineries, had even put a tax on American refined.

In the fall of 1871, while Mr. Rockefeller and his friends were occupied with all these questions, certain Pennsylvania refiners, it is not too certain who, brought to them a remarkable scheme, the gist of which was to bring together secretly a large enough body of refiners and shippers to persuade all the railroads handling oil to give to the company formed special rebates on its oil, and drawbacks on that of other people. If they could get such rates it was evident that those outside of their combination could not compete with them long and that they would become eventually the only refiners. They could then limit their output to actual demand, and so keep up prices. This done, they could easily persuade the railroads to transport no crude for exportation, so that the foreigners would be forced to buy American refined. They believed that the price of oil thus exported could easily be advanced fifty per cent. The control of the refining interests would also enable them to fix their own price on crude. As they would be the only buyers and sellers, the speculative character of the business would be done away with. In short, the scheme they worked out put the entire oil business in their hands. It looked as simple to put into operation as it was dazzling in its results. Mr. Flagler has sworn that neither he nor Mr. Rockefeller believed in this scheme. But when they found that their friend Peter H. Watson, and various Philadelphia and Pittsburgh parties who felt as they did about the oil business, believed in it, they went in and began at once to work up a company — secretly. It was evident that a scheme which aimed at concentrating in the hands of one company the business now operated by scores, and which proposed to effect this consolidation through a practice of the railroads which was contrary to the spirit of their charters, although freely indulged in, must be worked with fine discretion if it ever were to be effective.

The first thing was to get a charter — quietly. At a meeting held in Philadelphia late in the fall of 1871 a friend of one of the gentlemen interested mentioned to him that a certain estate then in liquidation had a charter for sale which gave its owners the right to carry on any kind of business in any country and in any way; that it could be bought for what it would cost to get a charter under the general laws of the state, and that it would be a favour to the heirs to buy it. The opportunity was promptly taken. The name of the charter bought was the "South (often written Southern) Improvement Company." For a beginning it was as good a name as another, since it said nothing.

With this charter in hand Mr. Rockefeller and Mr. Watson and their associates began to seek converts. In order that their great scheme might not be injured by premature public discussion they asked of each person whom they approached a pledge of secrecy. Two forms of the pledges required before anything was revealed were published later. The first of these, which appeared in the New York Tribune, read as follows:

I, A. B., do faithfully promise upon my honour and faith as a gentleman that I will keep secret all transactions which I may have with the corporation known as the South Improvement Company; that, should I fail to complete any bargains with the said company, all the preliminary conversations shall be kept strictly private; and, finally, that I will not disclose the price for which I dispose of my product, or any other facts which may in any way bring to light the internal workings or organisation of the company. All this I do freely promise.
Signed . . . .
Witnessed by . . . . — .

A second, published in a history of the "Southern Improvement Company," ran:

The undersigned pledge their solemn words of honour that they will not communicate to any one without permission of Z (name of director of Southern Improvement Company) any information that he may convey to them, or any of them, in relation to the Southern Improvement Company.

. . . .

Witness . . . .

That the promoters met with encouragement is evident from the fact that, when the corporators came together on January 2, 1872, in Philadelphia, for the first time under their charter, and transferred the company to the stockholders, they claimed to represent in one way or another a large part of the refining interest of the country. At this meeting 1,100 shares of the stock of the company, which was divided into 2,000 $100 shares, were subscribed for, and twenty per cent of their value was paid in. Just who took stock at this meeting the writer has not been able to discover. At the same time a discussion came up as to what refiners were to be allowed to go into the new company. Each of the men represented had friends whom he wanted taken care of, and after considerable discussion it was decided to take in every refinery they could get hold of. This decision was largely due to the railroad men. Mr. Watson had seen them as soon as the plans for the company were formed, and they had all agreed that if they gave the rebates and drawbacks all refineries then existing must be taken in upon the same level. That is, while the incorporators had intended to kill off all but themselves and their friends, the railroads refused to go into a scheme which was going to put anybody out of business — the plan if they went into it must cover the refining trade as it stood. It was enough that it could prevent any one in the future going into the business.

Very soon after this meeting on January 2 the rest of the stock of the South

Improvement Company was taken. The complete list of stockholders, with their holdings, was as follows:

	SHARES
William Frew, Philadelphia	10
W. P. Logan, Philadelphia	10
John P. Logan, Philadelphia	10
Charles Lockhart, Pittsburgh	10
Richard S. Waring, Pittsburgh	10
W. G. Warden, Philadelphia	475
O. F. Waring, Pittsburgh	475
P. H. Watson, Ashtabula, Ohio	100
H. M. Flagler, Cleveland	180
O. H. Payne, Cleveland	180
William Rockefeller, Cleveland	180
J. A. Bostwick, New York	180
John D. Rockefeller, Cleveland[4]	180
	2,000

Mr. Watson was elected president and W. G. Warden of Philadelphia secretary of the new association. It will be noticed that the largest individual holdings in the company were those of W. G. Warden and O. F. Waring, each of whom had 475 shares. The company most heavily interested in the South Improvement Company was the Standard Oil of Cleveland, J. D. Rockefeller, William Rockefeller and H. M. Flagler, all stockholders of that company, each having 180 shares — 540 in the company. O. H. Payne and J. A. Bostwick, who soon after became stockholders in the Standard Oil Company, also had each 180 shares, giving Mr. Rockefeller and his associates 900 shares in all.

It has frequently been stated that the South Improvement Company represented the bulk of the oil-refining interests in the country. The incorporators of the company in approaching the railroads

[4] List of stockholders given by W. G. Warden, secretary of the South Improvement Company, to a Congressional Investigating Committee which examined Mr. Warden and Mr. Watson in March and April, 1872.

assured them that this was so. As a matter of fact, however, the thirteen gentlemen above named, who were the only ones ever holding stock in the concern, did not control over one-tenth of the refining business of the United States in 1872. That business in the aggregate amounted to a daily capacity of about 45,000 barrels — from 45,000 to 50,000, Mr. Warden put it — and the stockholders of the South Improvement Company owned a combined capacity of not over 4,600 barrels. In assuring the railroads that they controlled the business, they were dealing with their hopes rather than with facts.

The organisation complete, there remained contracts to be made with the railroads. Three systems were to be interested: the Central, which, by its connection with the Lake Shore and Michigan Southern, ran directly into the Oil Regions; the Erie, allied with the Atlantic and Great Western, with a short line likewise tapping the heart of the region; and the Pennsylvania, with the connections known as the Allegheny Valley and Oil Creek Railroad. The persons to be won over were: W. H. Vanderbilt, of the Central; H. F. Clark, president of the Lake Shore and Michigan Southern; Jay Gould, of the Erie; General G. B. McClellan, president of the Atlantic and Great Western; and Tom Scott, of the Pennsylvania. There seems to have been little difficulty in persuading any of these persons to go into the scheme after they had been assured by the leaders that all of the refiners were to be taken in. This was a verbal condition, however, not found in the contracts they signed. This important fact Mr. Warden himself made clear when three months later he was on the witness stand before a committee of Congress appointed to look into the great scheme. "We had considerable discussion with the railroads," Mr. Warden said, "in regard to the matter of rebate on their charges for freight; they did not want to give us a rebate unless it was with the understanding that all the refineries should be brought into the arrangement and placed upon the same level."

Q. You say you made propositions to railroad companies, which they agreed to accept upon the condition that you could include all the refineries?

A. No, sir; I did not say that; I said that was the understanding when we discussed this matter with them; it was no proposition on our part; they discussed it, not in the form of a proposition that the refineries should be all taken in, but it was the intention and resolution of the company from the first that that should be the result; we never had any other purpose in the matter.

Q. In case you could take the refineries all in, the railroads proposed to give you a rebate upon their freight charges?

A. No, sir; it was not put in that form; we were to put the refineries all in upon the same terms; it was the understanding with the railroad companies that we were to have a rebate; there was no rebate given in consideration of our putting the companies all in, but we told them we would do it; the contract with the railroad companies was with us.

Q. But if you did form a company composed of the proprietors of all these refineries, you were to have a rebate upon your freight charges?

A. No; we were to have a rebate anyhow, but were to give all the refineries the privilege of coming in.

Q. You were to have the rebate whether they came in or not?

A. Yes, sir.

*   *   *

"What effect were these arrangements to have upon those who did not come into the combination . . . ?" asked the chairman.

"I do not think we ever took that question up," answered Mr. Warden.

A second objection to making a contract with the company came from Mr. Scott of the Pennsylvania road and Mr. Potts of the Empire Transportation Company. The substance of this objection was that the plan took no account of the oil producer — the man to whom the world owed the business. Mr. Scott was strong in his assertion that they could never succeed unless they took care of the producers. Mr. Warden objected strongly to forming a combination with them. "The interests of the producers were in one sense antagonistic to ours: one as the seller and the other as the buyer. We held in argument that the producers were abundantly able to take care of their own branch of the business if they took care of the quantity produced." So strongly did Mr. Scott argue, however, that finally the members of the South Improvement Company yielded, and a draft of an agreement, to be proposed to the producers, was drawn up in lead-pencil; it was never presented. It seems to have been used principally to quiet Mr. Scott.

The work of persuasion went on swiftly. By the 18th of January the president of the Pennsylvania road, J. Edgar Thompson, had put his signature to the contract, and soon after Mr. Vanderbilt and Mr. Clark signed for the Central system, and Jay Gould and General McClellan for the Erie. The contracts to which these gentlemen put their names fixed gross rates of freight from all *common points*, as the leading shipping points within the Oil Regions were called, to all the great refining and shipping centres — New York, Philadelphia, Baltimore, Pittsburgh and Cleveland. For example, the open rate on crude to New York was put at $2.56. On this price the South Improvement Company was allowed a rebate of $1.06 for its shipments; but it got not only this rebate, it was given in cash a like amount on each barrel of crude shipped by parties outside the combination.

The open rate from Cleveland to New York was two dollars, and fifty cents of this was turned over to the South Improvement Company, which at the same time received a rebate enabling it to ship for $1.50. Again, an independent refiner in Cleveland paid eighty cents a barrel to get his crude from the Oil Regions to his works, and the railroad sent forty cents of this money to the South Improvement Company. At the same time it cost the Cleveland refiner in the combination but forty cents to get his crude oil. Like drawbacks and rebates were given for all points — Pittsburgh, Philadelphia, Boston and Baltimore.

An interesting provision in the contracts was that full waybills of all petroleum shipped over the roads should each day be sent to the South Improvement Company. This, of course, gave them knowledge of just who was doing business outside of their company — of how much business he was doing, and with whom he was doing it. Not only were they to have full knowledge of the business of all shippers — they were to have access to all books of the railroads.

The parties to the contracts agreed that if anybody appeared in the business offering an equal amount of transportation, and having equal facilities for doing business with the South Improvement Company, the railroads might give them equal advantages in drawbacks and rebates, but to make such a miscarriage of the scheme doubly improbable each railroad was bound to co-operate as "far as it legally might to maintain the business of the South Improvement Company against injury by competition, and lower or raise the gross rates of transportation for such times and to such extent as

might be necessary to overcome the competition. The rebates and drawbacks to be varied *pari passu* with the gross rates."[5]

The reason given by the railroads in the contract for granting these extraordinary privileges was that the "magnitude and extent of the business and operations" purposed to be carried on by the South Improvement Company would greatly promote the interest of the railroads and make it desirable for them to encourage their undertaking. The evident advantages received by the railroad were a regular amount of freight, — the Pennsylvania was to have forty-five per cent. of the Eastbound shipments, the Erie and Central each 27½ per cent., while Westbound freight was to be divided equally between them — fixed rates, and freedom from the system of cutting which they had all found so harassing and disastrous. That is, the South Improvement Company, which was to include the entire refining capacity of the company, was to act as the evener of the oil business.[6]

It was on the second of January, 1872, that the organisation of the South Improvement Company was completed. The day before the Standard Oil Company of Cleveland increased its capital from $1,000,000 to $2,500,000, "all the stockholders of the company being present and voting therefor."[7] These stockholders were greater by five than in 1870, the names of O. B. Jennings, Benjamin Brewster, Truman P. Handy, Amasa Stone, and Stillman Witt having been

5 Article Fourth: Contracts between the South Improvement Company and the Pennsylvania Railroad Company, January 18, 1872.

6 . . . Contract between the South Improvement Company and the Pennsylvania Railroad Company. Dated January 18, 1872.

7 . . . Standard Oil Company's application for increase of capital stock to $2,500,000 in 1872.

added. The last three were officers and stockholders in one or more of the railroads centring in Cleveland. Three weeks after this increase of capital Mr. Rockefeller had the charter and contracts of the South Improvement Company in hand, and was ready to see what they would do in helping him carry out his idea of wholesale combination in Cleveland. There were at that time some twenty-six refineries in the town — some of them very large plants. All of them were feeling more or less the discouraging effects of the last three or four years of railroad discriminations in favour of the Standard Oil Company. To the owners of these refineries Mr. Rockefeller now went one by one, and explained the South Improvement Company. "You see," he told them, "this scheme is bound to work. It means an absolute control by us of the oil business. There is no chance for anyone outside. But we are going to give everybody a chance to come in. You are to turn over your refinery to my appraisers, and I will give you Standard Oil Company stock or cash, as you prefer, for the value we put upon it. I advise you to take the stock. It will be for your good." Certain refiners objected. They did not want to sell. They did want to keep and manage their business. Mr. Rockefeller was regretful, but firm. It was useless to resist, he told the hesitating; they would certainly be crushed if they did not accept his offer, and he pointed out in detail, and with gentleness, how beneficent the scheme really was — preventing the creek refiners from destroying Cleveland, ending competition, keeping up the price of refined oil, and eliminating speculation. Really a wonderful contrivance for the good of the oil business.

That such was Mr. Rockefeller's argument is proved by abundant testimony from different individuals who succumbed to the pressure. Mr. Rockefeller's own brother, Frank Rockefeller, gave most definite evidence on this point in 1876 when he and others were trying to interest Congress in a law regulating interstate commerce.

"We had in Cleveland at one time about thirty establishments, but the South Improvement Company was formed, and the Cleveland companies were told that if they didn't sell their property to them it would be valueless, that there was a combination of railroad and oil men, that they would buy all they could, and that all they didn't buy would be totally valueless, because they would be unable to compete with the South Improvement Company, and the result was that out of thirty there were only four or five that didn't sell."

"From whom was that information received?" asked the examiner.

"From the officers of the Standard Oil Company. They made no bones about it at all. They said; 'If you don't sell your property to us it will be valueless, because we have got advantages with the railroads.'"

"Have you heard those gentlemen say what you have stated?" Frank Rockefeller was asked.

"I have heard Rockefeller and Flagler say so," he answered.

W. H. Doane, whose evidence on the first rebates granted to the Cleveland trade we have already quoted, told the Congressional committee which a few months after Mr. Rockefeller's great coup tried to find out what happened in Cleveland: "The refineries are all bought up by the Standard Oil works; they were forced to sell; the railroads had put up the rates and it scared them. Men came to me and told me they could not continue their business; they became frightened and disposed of their property." Mr. Doane's own business, that of a crude oil shipper, was entirely ruined, all of his customers but one having sold.

To this same committee Mr. Alexander, of Alexander, Scofield and Company, gave his reason for selling:

"There was a pressure brought to bear upon my mind, and upon almost all citizens of Cleveland engaged in the oil business, to the effect that unless we went into the South Improvement Company we were virtually killed as refiners; that if we did not sell out we should be crushed out. My partner, Mr. Hewitt, had some negotiations with parties connected with the South Improvement Company, and they gave us to understand, at least my partner so represented to me, that we should be crushed out if we did not go into that arrangement. He wanted me to see the parties myself; but I said to him that I would not have any dealings with certain parties who were in that company for any purpose, and I never did. We sold at a sacrifice, and we were obliged to. There was only one buyer in the market, and we had to sell on their terms or be crushed out, as it was represented to us. It was stated that they had a contract with railroads by which they could run us into the ground if they pleased. After learning what the arrangements were I felt as if, rather than fight such a monopoly, I would withdraw from the business, even at a sacrifice. I think we received about forty or forty-five cents on the dollar on the valuation which we placed upon our refinery. We had spent over $50,000 on our works during the past year, which was nearly all that we received. We had paid out $60,000 or $70,000 before that; we considered our works at their cash value worth seventy-five per cent. of their cost. According to our valuation our establishment was worth $150,000, and we sold it for about $65,000, which was about forty or forty-five per cent. of its value. We sold to one of the members, as I suppose, of the South Improvement Company, Mr. Rockefeller; he is a director in that company; it was sold in name to the Standard Oil Company, of Cleveland, but the arrangements were, as I understand it, that they were to put it into the South Improvement Company. I am stating what my partner told me; he did all the business; his statement was that all these works were to be merged into the South Improvement Company. I never talked with any members of the South Improvement Company myself on the subject; I declined to have anything to do with them."

Mr. Hewitt, the partner who Mr. Alexander says carried on the negotiations for the sale of the business, appeared before an investigating committee of the New York State Senate in 1879 and gave his recollections of what happened. According to his story the entire oil trade in Cleveland became paralysed when it became known that the South Improvement Company had "grappled the entire transportation of oil from the West to the seaboard." Mr. Hewitt went to see the freight agents of the various roads; he called on W. H. Vanderbilt, but from no one did he get any encouragement. Then he saw Peter H. Watson of the Lake Shore Railroad, the president of the company which was frightening the trade. "Watson was non-committal," said Mr. Hewitt. "I got no satisfaction except, 'You better sell — you better get clear — better sell out — no help for it.'" After a little time Mr. Hewitt concluded with his partners that there was indeed "no help for it," and he went to see Mr. Rockefeller, who offered him fifty cents on the dollar on the constructive account. The offer was accepted. There was nothing else to do, the firm seems to have concluded. When they came to transfer the property Mr. Rockefeller urged Mr. Hewitt to take stock in the new concern. "He told me," said Mr. Hewitt, "that it would be sufficient to take care of my family for all time, what I represented there, and asking for a reason, he made this expression, I remember: '*I have ways of making money that you know nothing of.*'"

A few of the refiners contested before surrendering. Among these was Robert Hanna, an uncle of Mark Hanna, of the firm of Hanna, Baslington and Company. Mr. Hanna had been refining since July, 1869. According to his own sworn statement he had made money, fully sixty per cent. on his investment the first year, and after that thirty per cent. Some time in February, 1872, the Standard Oil Company asked an interview with him and his associates. They wanted to buy his works, they said. "But we don't want to sell," objected Mr. Hanna. "You can never make any more money, in my judgment," said Mr. Rockefeller. "You can't compete with the Standard. We have all the large refineries now. If you refuse to sell, it will end in your being crushed." Hanna and Baslington were not satisfied. They went to see Mr. Watson, president of the South Improvement Company and an officer of the Lake Shore, and General Devereux, manager of the Lake Shore road. They were told that the Standard had special rates; that it was useless to try to compete with them. General Devereux explained to the gentlemen that the privileges granted the Standard were the legitimate and necessary advantage of the larger shipper over the smaller, and that if Hanna, Baslington and Company could give the road as large a quantity of oil as the Standard did, with the same regularity, they could have the same rate. General Devereux says they "recognized the propriety" of his excuse. They certainly recognised its authority. They say that they were satisfied they could no longer get rates to and from Cleveland which would enable them to live, and "reluctantly" sold out.

It must have been reluctantly, for they had paid $75,000 for their works, and had made thirty per cent. a year on an average on their investment, and the Standard appraiser allowed them $45,000. "Truly and really less than one-half of what they were absolutely worth, with a fair and honest competition in the lines of transportation," said Mr. Hanna, eight years later, in an affidavit.

Under the combined threat and persuasion of the Standard, armed with the South Improvement Company scheme, almost the entire independent oil interest of Cleveland collapsed in three months' time. Of the twenty-six refineries, at least twenty-one sold out. From a capacity of probably not over 1,500 barrels of crude a day, the Standard Oil Company rose in three months' time to one of 10,000 barrels. By this manoeuvre it became master of over one-fifth of the refining capacity of the United States.[8] Its next individual competitor was Sone and Fleming, of New York, whose capacity was 1,700 barrels. The Standard had a greater capacity than the entire Oil Creek Regions, greater than the combined New York refiners. The transaction by which it acquired this power was so stealthy that not even the best informed newspaper men of Cleveland knew what went on. It had all been accomplished in ac-

[8] In 1872 the refining capacity of the United States was as follows, according to Henry's "Early and Later History of Petroleum":

	BARRELS
Oil Regions	9,231
New York	9,790
Cleveland	12,732
Pittsburgh	6,090
Philadelphia	2,061
Baltimore	1,098
Boston	3,500
Erie	1,168
Other Points	901
Total	46,571

cordance with one of Mr. Rockefeller's chief business principles — "Silence is golden.". . .

Few men in either the political or industrial life of this country can point to an achievement carried out in more exact accord with its first conception than John D. Rockefeller, for both in purpose and methods the Standard Oil Company is and always has been a form of the South Improvement Company, by which Mr. Rockefeller first attracted general attention in the oil industry. The original scheme has suffered many modifications. Its most offensive feature, the drawback on other people's shipments, has been cut off. Nevertheless, today, as at the start, the purpose of the Standard Oil Company is the purpose of the South Improvement Company — the regulation of the price of crude and refined oil by the control of the output; and the chief means for sustaining this purpose is still that of the original scheme — a control of oil transportation giving special privileges in rates.

It is now thirty-two years since Mr. Rockefeller applied the fruitful idea of the South Improvement Company to the Standard Oil Company of Ohio, a prosperous oil refinery of Cleveland, with a capital of $1,000,000 and a daily capacity for handling 1,500 barrels of crude oil. And what have we as a result? What is the Standard Oil Company to-day? First, what is its organisation? It is no longer a trust. As we have seen, the trust was obliged to liquidate in 1892. It became a "trust in liquidation," and there it remained for some five years. In 1898, when the possibility arose . . . of the state of Ohio taking away the charters of four of its important constituent companies for contempt of court and violation of the anti-trust laws of the state, [its only

refuge] lay in the corporation law of the state of New Jersey, which had just been amended, and here it settled. Among the twenty companies which formed the trust was the Standard Oil Company of New Jersey, a corporation for manufacturing and marketing petroleum products. Its capital was $10,000,000. In June, 1899, this capital of $10,000,000 was increased to one of $110,000,000, and into this new organisation was dumped the entire Standard aggregation. The old trust certificates outstanding and the assignments of legal title which had succeeded them were called in, and for them was given common stock of the new Standard Oil Company. The amount of this stock which had been issued, in January, 1904, when the last report was made, was $97,448,800. Its market value at that date was $643,162,080. How it is divided is of course a matter of private concern. The number of stockholders in 1899 was about 3,500, according to Mr. Archbold's testimony to the Interstate Commerce Commission, but over one-half of the stock was owned by the directors, and probably nearly one-third was owned by Mr. Rockefeller himself.

The companies which this new Standard Oil Company has bought up with its stock are numerous and scattered. They consist of oil-producing companies like the South Penn Oil Company, the Ohio Oil Company, and the Forest Oil Company; of transporting companies like the National Transit Company, the Buckeye Pipe Line Company, the Indiana Pipe Line Company, and the Eureka Pipe Line Company; of manufacturing and marketing companies like the Atlantic Refining Company of Pennsylvania, and the Standard Oil Companies of many states — New York, Indiana, Kentucky, Ohio, Iowa; of foreign marketing concerns like the Anglo-American Company.

In 1892 there were twenty of these constituent companies. There have been many added since, in whole or part, like gas companies; new producing concerns, made necessary by developments in California, Kansas and Texas; new marketing concerns for handling oil directly in Germany, Italy, Scandinavia and Portugal. What the total value of the companies owned by the present Standard Oil Company is it is impossible to say. In 1892, when the trust was on trial in Ohio, it reported the aggregate capital of its twenty companies as $102,233,700, and the appraised value was given as $121,631,312.63; that is, there was an excess of about $19,000,000.

In 1898, when Attorney-General Monnett of Ohio had the Standard Oil Company of the state on trial for contempt of court, he tried to find out from Mr. Rockefeller what the surplus of each of the various companies in the trust was at that date. Mr. Rockefeller answered: "I have not in my possession or power data showing . . . the amount of such surplus money in their hands after the payment of the last dividends." Then Mr. Rockefeller proceeded to repeat as the last he knew of the value of the holdings of the trust the list of values given six years before. This list has continued to be cited ever since as authoritative. There is a later one, whether Mr. Rockefeller had it in his "possession or power," or not, in 1898. It is the last trustworthy valuation of which the writer knows, and is found in testimony taken in 1899, in a private suit to which Mr. Rockefeller was party. It is for the year 1896. This shows the "total capital and surplus" of the twenty companies to have been, on December 31 of that year, something over one hundred and forty-seven million dollars, nearly forty-nine millions of which was scheduled as "undivided

profits." Of course there has been a constant increase in value since 1896.

The new Standard Oil Company is managed by a board of fourteen directors. They probably collect the dividends of the constituent companies and divide them among stockholders in exactly the same way the trustees of 1882 and the liquidating trustees of 1892 did. As for the charter under which they are operating, never since the days of the South Improvement Company has Mr. Rockefeller held privileges so in harmony with his ambition. By it he can do all kinds of mining, manufacturing, and trading business; transport goods and merchandise by land and water in any manner; buy, sell, lease, and improve lands; build houses, structures, vessels, cars, wharves, docks, and piers; lay and operate pipelines; erect and operate telegraph and telephone lines, and lines for conducting electricity; enter into and carry out contracts of every kind pertaining to his business; acquire, use, sell, and grant licenses under patent rights; purchase, or otherwise acquire, hold, sell, assign, and transfer shares of capital stock and bonds or other evidences of indebtedness of corporations, and exercise all the privileges of ownership, including voting upon the stocks so held; carry on its business and have offices and agencies therefor in all parts of the world, and hold, purchase, mortgage, and convey real estate and personal property outside the state of New Jersey. These privileges are, of course, subject to the laws of the state or country in which the company operates. If it is contrary to the laws of a state for a foreign corporation to hold real estate in its boundaries, a company must be chartered in the state. Its stock, of course, is sold to the New Jersey corporation, so that it amounts to the same thing as far as the ability to do business is concerned. It will be seen that this really amounts to a special charter allowing the holder not only to do all that is specified, but to create whatever other power it desires, except banking. A comparison of this summary of powers with those granted by the South Improvement Company shows that in sweep of charter, at least, the Standard Oil Company of to-day has as great power as its famous progenitor.

The profits of the present Standard Oil Company are enormous. For five years the dividends have been averaging about forty-five million dollars a year, or nearly fifty per cent. on its capitalisation, a sum which capitalised at five per cent. would give $900,000,000. Of course this is not all that the combination makes in a year. It allows an annual average of 5.77 per cent. for deficit, and it carries always an ample reserve fund. When we remember that probably one-third of this immense annual revenue goes into the hands of John D. Rockefeller, that probably ninety per cent. of it goes to the few men who make up the "Standard Oil family," and that it must every year be invested, the Standard Oil Company becomes a much more serious public matter than it was in 1872, when it stamped itself as willing to enter into a conspiracy to raid the oil business — as a much more serious concern than in the years when it openly made warfare of business, and drove from the oil industry by any means it could invent all who had the hardihood to enter it. For, consider what must be done with the greater part of this $45,000,000. It must be invested. The oil business does not demand it. There is plenty of reserve for all of its ventures. It must go into other industries. Naturally, the interests sought will be allied to oil. They will be gas, and we have the Standard Oil crowd steadily acquir-

ing the gas interests of the country. They will be railroads, for on transportation all industries depend, and, besides, railroads are one of the great consumers of oil products and must be kept in line as buyers. And we have the directors of the Standard Oil Company acting as directors on nearly all of the great railways of the country, the New York Central, New York, New Haven and Hartford, Chicago, Milwaukee and St. Paul, Union Pacific, Northern Pacific, Delaware, Lackawanna and Western, Missouri Pacific, Missouri, Kansas and Texas, Boston and Maine, and other lesser roads. They will go into copper, and we have the Amalgamated scheme. They will go into steel, and we have Mr. Rockefeller's enormous holdings in the Steel Trust. They will go into banking, and we have the National City Bank and its allied institutions in New York City and Boston, as well as a long chain running over the country. No one who has followed this history can expect these holdings will be acquired on a rising market. Buy cheap and sell high is a rule of business, and when you control enough money and enough banks you can always manage that a stock you want shall be temporarily cheap. No value is destroyed for you — only for the original owner. This has been one of Mr. Rockefeller's most successful manoeuvres in doing business from the day he scared his twenty Cleveland competitors until they sold to him at half price. You can also sell high, if you have a reputation of a great financier, and control of money and banks. Amalgamated Copper is an excellent example. The names of certain Standard Oil officials would float the most worthless property on earth a few years ago. It might be a little difficult for them to do so to-day with Amalgamated so fresh in mind. Indeed,

Amalgamated seems to-day to be the worst "break," as it certainly was one of the most outrageous performances of the Standard Oil crowd. But that will soon be forgotten! The result is that the Standard Oil Company is probably in the strongest financial position of any aggregation in the world. And every year its position grows stronger, for every year there is pouring in another $45,000,000 to be used in wiping up the property most essential to preserving and broadening its power.

And now what does the law of New Jersey require the concern which it has chartered, and which is so rapidly adding to its control of oil the control of iron, steel, copper, banks, and railroads, to make known of itself? It must each year report its name, the location of its registration office, with name of agent, the character of its business, the amount of capital stock issued, and the names and addresses of its officers and directors!

So much for present organisation, and now as to how far through this organisation the Standard Oil Company is able to realise the purpose for which it was organised — the control of the output, and, through that, the price, of refined oil. That is, what per cent. of the whole oil business does Mr. Rockefeller's concern control. First as to oil production. In 1898 the Standard Oil Company reported to the Industrial Commission that it produced 35.58 per cent. of Eastern crude — the production that year was about 52,000,000 barrels. (It should be remembered that it is always to the Eastern oil fields — Pennsylvania, Ohio, Indiana, West Virginia — that this narrative refers. Texas, Kansas, Colorado and California are newer developments. These fields have not as yet been determining factors in the business, though Texas particularly has been a distribut-

ing factor.) But while Mr. Rockefeller produces only about a third of the entire production, he controls all but about ten per cent. of it; that is, all but about ten per cent. goes immediately into his custody on coming from the wells. It passes entirely out of the hands of the producers when the Standard pipe-line takes it. The oil is in Mr. Rockefeller's hands, and he, not the producer, can decide who is to have it. The greater portion of it he takes himself, of course, for he is the chief refiner of the country. In 1898 there were about twenty-four million barrels of petroleum products made in this country. Of this amount about twenty million were made by the Standard Oil Company; fully a third of the balance was produced by the Tidewater Company, of which the Standard holds a large minority stock, and which for twenty years has had a running arrangement with the Standard. Reckoning out the Tidewater's probable output, and we have an independent output of about 2,500,000 in twenty-four million. It is obvious that this great percentage of the business gives the Standard the control of prices. This control can be kept in the domestic markets so long as the Standard can keep under competition as successfully as it has in the past. It can be kept in the foreign market as long as American oils can be made and sold in quantity cheaper than foreign oils. . . .

Altogether the most important question concerning the Standard Oil Company to-day is how far it is sustaining its power by the employment of the peculiar methods of the South Improvement Company. It should never be forgotten that Mr. Rockefeller never depended on these methods alone for securing power in the oil trade. From the beginning the Standard Oil Company has studied thoroughly everything connected with the oil business. It has known, not guessed at, conditions. It has had a keen authoritative sight. It has applied itself to its tasks with indefatigable zeal. It has been as courageous as it has been cautious. Nothing has been too big to undertake, as nothing has been too small to neglect. These facts have been repeatedly pointed out in this narrative. But these are the American industrial qualities. They are common enough in all sorts of business. They have made our railroads, built up our great department stores, opened our mines. The Standard Oil Company has no monopoly in business ability. It is the thing for which American men are distinguished to-day in the world.

These qualities alone would have made a great business, and unquestionably it would have been along the line of combination, for when Mr. Rockefeller undertook to work out the good of the oil business the tendency to combination was marked throughout the industry, but it would not have been the combination whose history we have traced. To the help of these qualities Mr. Rockefeller proposed to bring the peculiar aids of the South Improvement Company. He secured an alliance with the railroads to drive out rivals. For fifteen years he received rebates of varying amounts on at least the greater part of his shipments, and for at least a portion of that time he collected drawbacks of the oil other people shipped; at the same time he worked with the railroads to prevent other people getting oil to manufacture, or if they got it he worked with the railroads to prevent the shipment of the product. If it reached a dealer, he did his utmost to bully or wheedle him to countermand his order. If he failed in that, he undersold until the dealer, losing on his purchase, was glad enough to buy thereafter of Mr. Rockefeller. How much

of this system remains in force to-day? The spying on independent shipments, the effort to have orders countermanded, the predatory competition prevailing, are well enough known. Contemporaneous documents, showing how these practices have been worked into a very perfect and practically universal system, have already been printed in this work. As for the rebates and drawbacks, if they do not exist in the forms practised up to 1887, as the Standard officials have repeatedly declared, it is not saying that the Standard enjoys no special transportation privileges. As has been pointed out, it controls the great pipe-line handling all but perhaps ten per cent. of the oil produced in the Eastern fields. This system is fully 35,000 miles long. It goes to the wells of every producer, gathers his oil into its storage tanks, and from there transports it to Philadelphia, Baltimore, New York, Chicago, Buffalo, Cleveland, or any other refining point where it is needed. This pipe-line is a common carrier by virtue of its use of the right of eminent domain, and, as a common carrier, is theoretically obliged to carry and deliver the oil of all comers, but in practice this does not always work. It has happened more than once in the history of the Standard pipes that they have refused to gather or deliver oil. Pipes have been taken up from wells belonging to individuals running or working with independent refiners. Oil has been refused delivery at points practical for independent refiners. For many years the supply of oil has been so great that the Standard could not refuse oil to the independent refiner on the ground of scarcity. However, a shortage in Pennsylvania oil occurred in 1903. A very interesting situation arose as a result. There are in Ohio and Pennsylvania several independent refiners who, for a number of years, have depended on the Standard lines (the National Transit Company) for their supply of crude. In the fall of 1903 these refiners were informed that thereafter the Standard could furnish them with only fifty per cent. of their refining capacity. It was a serious matter to the independents, who had their own markets, and some of whom were increasing their plants. Supposing we buy oil directly from the producers, they asked one another, must not the Standard as a common carrier gather and deliver it? The experienced in the business said: "Yes. But what will happen? The producer rash enough to sell you oil may be cut off by the National Transit Company. Of course, if he wants to fight in the courts he may eventually force the Standard to reconnect, but they could delay the suit until he was ruined. Also, if you go over Mr. Seep's head" — Mr. Seep is the Standard Oil buyer, and all oil going into the National Transit system goes through his hands — "you will antagonise him." Now, "antagonise" in Standard circles may mean a variety of things. The independent refiners decided to compromise, and an agreement terminable by either party at short notice was made between them and the Standard, by which the members of the former were each to have eighty per cent. of their capacity of crude oil, and were to give to the Standard all of their export oil to market. As a matter of fact, the Standard's ability to cut off crude supplies from the outside refiners is much greater than in the days before the Interstate Commerce Bill, when it depended on its alliance with the railroads to prevent its rival getting oil. It goes without saying that this is an absurd power to allow in the hands of any manufacturer of a great necessity of life. It is exactly as if one corporation aiming at

manufacturing all the flour of the country owned all but ten per cent. of the entire railroad system collecting and transporting wheat. They could, of course, in time of shortage, prevent any would-be competitor from getting grain to grind, and they could and would make it difficult and expensive at all times for him to get it.

It is not only in the power of the Standard to cut off outsiders from it, it is able to keep up transportation prices. Mr. Rockefeller owns the pipe system — a common carrier — and the refineries of the Standard Oil Company pay in the final accounting cost for transporting their oil, while outsiders pay just what they paid twenty-five years ago. There are lawyers who believe that if this condition were tested in the courts, the National Transit Company would be obliged to give the same rates to others as the Standard refineries ultimately pay. It would be interesting to see the attempt made.

Not only are outside refiners at just as great disadvantage in securing crude supply to-day as before the Interstate Commerce Commission was formed; they still suffer severe discrimination on the railroads in marketing their product. There are many ways of doing things. What but discrimination is the situation which exists in the comparative rates for oil freight between Chicago and New Orleans, and Cleveland and New Orleans? All, or nearly all, of the refined oil sold by the Standard Oil Company through the Mississippi Valley and the West is manufactured at Whiting, Indiana, close to Chicago, and is shipped on Chicago rates. There are no important independent oil works at Chicago. Now at Cleveland, Ohio, there are independent refiners and jobbers contending for the market of the Mississippi Valley. See how prettily it is managed. The rates between the two Northern cities and New Orleans in the case of nearly all commodities is about two cents per hundred pounds in favour of Chicago. For example, the rate on flour from Chicago is 23 cents per 100 pounds; from Cleveland, 25 cents per 100 pounds; on canned goods the rates are 33 and 35; on lumber, 31 and 33; on meats, 51 and 54; on all sorts of iron and steel, 26 and 29; but on petroleum and its products they are 23 and 33! . . . [Miss Tarbell lists other examples, omitted here.]

Examples of this manipulation might be multiplied. There is no independent refiner or jobber who tries to ship oil freight that does not meet incessant discouragement and discrimination. Not only are rates made to favour the Standard refining points and to protect their markets, but switching charges and dock charges are multiplied. Loading and unloading facilities are refused, payment of freights on small quantities are demanded in advance, a score of different ways are found to make hard the way of the outsider. "If I get a barrel of oil out of Buffalo," an independent dealer told the writer not long ago, "I have to *sneak* it out. There are no public docks; the railroads control most of them, and they won't let me out if they can help it. If I want to ship a car-load they won't take it if they can help it. They are all afraid of offending the Standard Oil Company."

This may be a rather sweeping statement, but there is too much truth in it. There is no doubt that to-day, as before the Interstate Commerce Commission, a community of interests exists between railroads and the Standard Oil Company sufficiently strong for the latter to get any help it wants in making it hard for rivals to do business. The Standard owns stock in most of the great systems. It is represented on the board of directors of nearly all the great systems, and it has an immense freight not only in oil products, but in timber, iron, acids, and all of the necessities of its factories. It is allied with many other industries, iron, steel, and copper, and can swing freight away from a road which does not oblige it. It has great influence in the money market and can help or hinder a road in securing money. It has great influence in the stock market and can depress or inflate a stock if it sets about it. Little wonder that the railroads, being what they are, are afraid to "disturb their relations with the Standard Oil Company," or that they keep alive a system of discrimination the same in effect as those which existed before 1887.

Of course such cases as those cited above are fit for the Interstate Commerce Commission, but the oil men as a body have no faith in the effectiveness of an appeal to the Commission, and in this feeling they do not reflect on the Commission, but rather on the ignorance and timidity of the Congress which, after creating a body which the people demanded, made it helpless. The case on which the Oil Regions rests its reason for its opinion has already been referred to in the chapter on the co-operative independent movement which finally resulted in the Pure Oil Company. The case first came before the Commission in 1888. At that time there was a small group of independent refiners in Oil City and Titusville, who were the direct outgrowth of the compromise of 1880 between the Producers' Protective Association and the Pennsylvania Railroad. The railroad, having promised open rates to all, urged the men to go into business. Soon after came the great fight between the railroads and the seaboard pipe-line, with the consequent low rates. This warfare finally ended in 1884, after the Standard had brought the Tidewater into line, in a pooling arrangement between the Standard, now controlling all seaboard pipe-lines, and the Pennsylvania Railroad, by which the latter was guaranteed twenty-six per cent. of all Eastern oil shipments on condition that they keep up the rate to the seaboard to fifty-two cents a barrel.

Now, most of the independents shipped by barrels loaded on rack cars. The Standard shipped almost entirely by tank-cars. The custom had always been in the Oil Regions to charge the same for shipments whether by tank or barrel. Suddenly, in 1888, the rate of fifty-two cents on oil in barrels was raised to one of sixty-six cents. The independents believed that the raise was a manipulation of the Standard intended to kill their export trade, and they appealed to the Commission. They pointed out that the railroads and the pipe-lines had been keeping up rates for a long time by a pooling arrangement, and that now the roads made an unreasonable tariff on oil in barrels, at the same time refusing them tank cars. The hearing took place in Titusville in May, 1889. The railroads argued that they had advanced the rate on barrelled oil because of a decision of the Commission itself — a case of very evident discrimination in favour of barrels. The Commission, however, argued that each case brought before it must stand on its own merits, so different were conditions and practices, and in December, 1892, it gave its decision. The pooling arrangement it did not touch, on the ground that the Commission had authority only over railroads in competition, not over railroads and pipe-lines in competition. The chief complaint, that the new rate of sixty-six cents on oil in bar-

rels and not on oil in tanks was an injurious discrimination, the Commission found justified. It ordered that the railroads make the rates the same on oil in both tanks and barrels, and that they furnish shippers tanks whenever reasonable notice was given. As the amounts wrongfully collected by the railroads from the refiners could not be ascertained from the evidence already taken, the Commission decided to hold another hearing and fix the amounts. This was not done until May, 1894, five years after the first hearing. Reparation was ordered to at least eleven different firms, some of the sums amounting to several thousand dollars; the entire award ordered amounted to nearly $100,000.

In case the railroads failed to adjust the claims the refiners were ordered to proceed to enforce them in the courts. The Commission found at this hearing that none of their orders of 1892 had been followed by the roads and they were all repeated. As was to be expected, the roads refused to recognise the claims allowed by the Commission, and the case was taken by the refiners into court. It has been heard three times. Twice they have won, but each time an appeal of the roads has forced them to appear again. The case was last heard at Philadelphia in February, 1904, in the United States Circuit Court of Appeals. No decision had been rendered at this writing.

It would be impossible to offer direct and conclusive proof that the Standard Oil Company persuaded or forced the roads to the change of policy complained of in this case, but the presence of their leading officials and counsel at the hearings, the number of witnesses furnished from their employ, the statement of President Roberts of the Pennsylvania Railroad that the raise on barrelled oil was insisted on by the seaboard refiners (the Standard was then practically the only seaboard refiner), as well as the perfectly well-known relations of the railroad and the Standard, left no doubt in the minds of those who knew the situation that the order originated with them, and that its sole purpose was harassing their competitors. The Commission seems to have had no doubt of this. But see the helplessness of the Commission. It takes full testimony in 1889, digests it carefully, gives its orders in 1892, and they are not obeyed. More hearings follow, and in 1895 the orders are repeated and reparation is allowed to the injured refiners. From that time to this the case passes from court to court, the railroad seeking to escape the Commission's orders. The Interstate Commerce Commission was instituted to facilitate justice in this matter of transportation, and yet here we have still unsettled a case on which they gave their judgment twelve years ago. The lawyer who took the first appeal to the Commission, that of Rice, Robinson and Winthrop, of Titusville, M. J. Heywang, of Titusville, has been continually engaged in the case for sixteen years!

In spite of the Interstate Commerce Commission, the crucial question is still a transportation question. Until the people of the United States have solved the question of free and equal transportation it is idle to suppose that they will not have a trust question. So long as it is possible for a company to own the exclusive carrier on which a great natural product depends for transportation, and to use this carrier to limit a competitor's supply or to cut off that supply entirely if the rival is offensive, and always to make him pay a higher rate than it costs the owner, it is ignorance and folly to talk about constitutional amendments

limiting trusts. So long as the great manufacturing centres of a monopolistic trust can get better rates than the centres of independent effort, it is idle to talk about laws making it a crime to undersell for the purpose of driving a competitor from a market. You must get into markets before you can compete. So long as railroads can be persuaded to interfere with independent pipe-lines, to refuse oil freight, to refuse loading facilities, lest they disturb their relations with the Standard Oil Company, it is idle to talk about investigations or anti-trust legislation or application of the Sherman law. So long as the Standard Oil Company can control transportation as it does today, it will remain master of the oil industry, and the people of the United States will pay for their indifference and folly in regard to transportation a good sound tax on oil, and they will yearly see an increasing concentration of natural resources and transportation systems in the Standard Oil crowd.

If all the country had suffered from these raids on competition, had been the limiting of the business opportunity of a few hundred men and a constant higher price for refined oil, the case would be serious enough, but there is a more serious side to it. The ethical cost of all this is the deep concern. We are a commercial people. We cannot boast of our arts, our crafts, our cultivation; our boast is in the wealth we produce. As a consequence business success is sanctified, and, practically, any methods which achieve it are justified by a larger and larger class. All sorts of subterfuges and sophistries and slurring over of facts are employed to explain aggregations of capital whose determining factor has been like that of the Standard Oil Company, special privileges obtained by persistent secret effort in opposition to the spirit of the law, the efforts of legislators, and the most outspoken public opinion. How often does one hear it argued, the Standard Oil Company is simply an inevitable result of economic conditions; that is, given the practices of the oil-bearing railroads in 1872 and the elements of speculation and the over-refining in the oil business, there was nothing for Mr. Rockefeller to do but secure special privileges if he wished to save his business.

Now in 1872 Mr. Rockefeller owned a successful refinery in Cleveland. He had the advantage of water transportation a part of the year, access to two great trunk lines the year around. Under such able management as he could give it his concern was bound to go on, given the demand for refined oil. It was bound to draw other firms to it. When he went into the South Improvement Company it was not to save his own business, but to destroy others. When he worked so persistently to secure rebates after the breaking up of the South Improvement Company, it was in the face of an industry united against them. It was not to save his business that he compelled the Empire Transportation Company to go out of the oil business in 1877. Nothing but grave mismanagement could have destroyed his business at that moment; it was to get every refinery in the country but his own out of the way. It was not the necessity to save his business which compelled Mr. Rockefeller to make war on the Tidewater. He and the Tidewater could both have lived. It was to prevent prices of transportation and of refined oil going down under competition. What necessity was there for Mr. Rockefeller trying to prevent the United States Pipe Line doing business? — only the greed of power and money. Every great campaign against rival interests

which the Standard Oil Company has carried on has been inaugurated, not to save its life, but to build up and sustain a monopoly in the oil industry. These are not mere affirmations of a hostile critic; they are facts proved by documents and figures.

Certain defenders go further and say that if some such combination had not been formed the oil industry would have failed for lack of brains and capital. Such a statement is puerile. Here was an industry for whose output the whole world was crying. Petroleum came at the moment when the value and necessity of a new, cheap light was recognized everywhere. Before Mr. Rockefeller had ventured outside of Cleveland kerosene was going in quantities to every civilised country. Nothing could stop it, nothing check it, but the discovery of some cheaper light or the putting up of its price. The real "good of the oil business" in 1872 lay in making oil cheaper. It would flow all over the world on its own merit if cheap enough.

The claim that only by some such aggregation as Mr. Rockefeller formed could enough capital have been obtained to develop the business falls utterly in face of fact. Look at the enormous amounts of capital, a large amount of it speculative, to be sure, which the oil men claim went into their business in the first ten years. It was estimated that Philadelphia alone put over $168,000,000 into the development of the Oil Regions, and New York $134,000,000, in their first decade of the business. How this estimate was reached the authority for it does not say.[9] It may have been the total capitalisation of the various oil companies launched in the two cities in that period. It shows very well, however, in what sort of figures the oil men were

9 The Petroleum Age, Volume I, page 35.

dealing. When the South Improvement Company trouble came in 1872, the producers launched a statement in regard to the condition of their business in which they claimed that they were using a capital of $200,000,000. Figures based on the number of oil wells in operation or drilling at that time of course represent only a portion of the capital in use. Wildcatting and speculation have always demanded a large amount of the money that the oil men handled. The almost conservative figures in regard to the capital invested in the Oil Regions in the early years were those of H. E. Wrigley, of the Geological Survey of Pennsylvania. Mr. Wrigley estimates that in the first twelve years of the business $235,000,000 was received from the wells. This includes the cost of the land, of putting down and operating the well, also the profit on the product. This estimate, however, makes no allowance for the sums used in speculation — an estimate, indeed, which it was impossible for one to make with any accuracy. The figures, unsatisfactory as they are, are ample proof, however, that there was plenty of money in the early days to carry on the oil business. Indeed, there has always been plenty of money for oil investment. It did not require Mr. Rockefeller's capital to develop the Bradford oil fields, build the first seaboard pipe-line, open West Virginia, Texas, or Kansas. The oil business would no more have suffered for lack of capital without the Standard combination than the iron or wheat or railroad or cotton business. The claim is idle, given the wealth and energy of the country in the forty-five years since the discovery of oil.

Equally well does both the history and the present condition of the oil business show that it has not needed any such aggregation to give us cheap oil. The margin between crude and refined was made low by competition. It has rarely been as low as it would have been had there been free competition. For five years even the small independent refineries outside of the Pure Oil Company have been able to make a profit on the prices set by the Standard, and this in spite of the higher transportation they have paid on both crude and refined, and the wall of seclusion the railroads build around domestic markets.

Very often people who admit the facts, who are willing to see that Mr. Rockefeller has employed force and fraud to secure his ends, justify him by declaring, "It's business." That is, "it's business" has come to be a legitimate excuse for hard dealing, sly tricks, special privileges. It is a common enough thing to hear men arguing that the ordinary laws of morality do not apply in business. Now, if the Standard Oil Company were the only concern in the country guilty of the practices which have given it monopolistic power, this story never would have been written. Were it alone in these methods, public scorn would long ago have made short work of the Standard Oil Company. But it is simply the most conspicuous type of what can be done by these practices. The methods it employs with such acumen, persistency, and secrecy are employed by all sorts of business men, from corner grocers up to bankers. If exposed, they are excused on the ground that this is business. If the point is pushed, frequently the defender of the practice falls back on the Christian doctrine of charity, and points that we are erring mortals and must allow for each other's weaknesses! — an excuse which, if carried to its legitimate conclusion, would leave our business men weeping on one another's shoulders over human frailty, while they picked one another's pockets.

One of the most depressing features of the ethical side of the matter is that instead of such methods arousing contempt they are more or less openly admired. And this is logical. Canonise "business success," and men who make a success like that of the Standard Oil Trust become national heroes! The history of its organisation is studied as a practical lesson in money-making. It is the most startling feature of the case to one who would like to feel that it is possible to be a commercial people and yet a race of gentlemen. Of course such practices exclude men by all the codes from the rank of gentlemen, just as such practices would exclude men from the sporting world or athletic field. There is no gaming table in the world where loaded dice are tolerated, no athletic field where men must not start fair. Yet Mr. Rockefeller has systematically played with loaded dice, and it is doubtful if there has ever been a time since 1872 when he has run a race with a competitor and started fair. Business played in this way loses all its sportsmanlike qualities. It is fit only for tricksters.

The effects on the very men who fight these methods on the ground that they are ethically wrong are deplorable. Brought into competition with the trust, badgered, foiled, spied upon, they come to feel as if anything is fair when the Standard is the opponent. The bitterness against the Standard Oil Company in many parts of Pennsylvania and Ohio is such that a verdict from a jury on the merits of the evidence is almost impossible! A case in point occurred a few years ago in the Bradford field. An oil producer was discovered stealing oil from the National Transit Company. He had tapped the main line and for at least two years had run a small but steady stream of Standard oil into his private tank. Finally the thieving pipe was discovered, and the owner of it, after acknowledging his guilt, was brought to trial. The jury gave a verdict of Not guilty! They seemed to feel that though the guilt was acknowledged, there probably was a Standard trick concealed somewhere. Anyway it was the Standard Oil Company and it deserved to be stolen from! The writer has frequently heard men, whose own business was conducted with scrupulous fairness, say in cases of similar stealing that they would never condemn a man who stole from the Standard! Of course such a state of feeling undermines the whole moral nature of a community.

The blackmailing cases of which the Standard Oil Company complains are a natural result of its own practices. Men going into an independent refining business have for years been accustomed to say: "Well, if they won't let us alone, we'll make them pay a good price." The Standard complains that such men build simply to sell out. There may be cases of this. Probably there are, though the writer has no absolute proof of any such. Certainly there is no satisfactory proof that the refinery in the famous Buffalo case was built to sell, though that it was offered for sale when the opposition of the Everests, the managers of the Standard concern, had become so serious as later to be stamped as criminal by judge and jury, there is no doubt. Certainly nothing was shown to have been done or said by Mr. Matthews, the owner of the concern which the Standard was fighting, which might not have been expected from a man who had met the kind of opposition he had from the time he went into business.

The truth is, blackmail and every other business vice is the natural result of the peculiar business practices of the Standard. If business is to be treated as warfare and not as a peaceful pursuit, as they have persisted in treating it, they cannot expect the men they are fighting to lie down and die without a struggle. If they get special privileges they must expect their competitors to struggle to get them. If they will find it more profitable to buy out a refinery than to let it live, they must expect the owner to get an extortionate price if he can. And when they complain of these practices and call them blackmail, they show thin sporting blood. They must not expect to monopolise hard dealings, if they do oil.

These are considerations of the ethical effect of such business practices on those outside and in competition. As for those within the organisation there is one obvious effect worth nothing. The Standard men as a body have nothing to do with public affairs, except as it is necessary to manipulate them for the "good of the oil business." The notion that the business man must not appear in politics and religion save as a "stand-patter" — not even as a thinking, aggressive force — is demoralising, intellectually and morally. Ever since 1872 the organisation has appeared in politics only to oppose legislation obviously for the public good. At that time the oil industry was young, only twelve years old, and it was suffering from too rapid growth, from speculation, from rapacity of railroads, but it was struggling manfully with all these questions. The question of railroad discriminations and extortions was one of the "live questions" of the country. The oil men as a mass were allied against it. The theory that the railroad was a public servant bound by the spirit of its charter to treat all shippers alike, that fair play demanded open equal rates to all, was generally held in the oil country at the time Mr. Rockefeller and his friends

sprung the South Improvement Company. One has only to read the oil journals at the time of the Oil War of 1872 to see how seriously all phases of the transportation question were considered. The country was a unit against the rebate system. Agreements were signed with the railroads that all rates henceforth should be equal. The signatures were not on before Mr. Rockefeller had a rebate, and gradually others got them until the Standard had won the advantages it expected the South Improvement Company to give it. From that time to this Mr. Rockefeller has had to fight the best sentiment of the oil country and of the country at large as to what is for the public good. He and his colleagues kept a strong alliance in Washington fighting the Interstate Commerce Bill from the time the first one was introduced in 1876 until the final passage in 1887. Every measure looking to the freedom and equalisation of transportation has met his opposition, as have bills for giving greater publicity to the operations of corporations. In many of the great state Legislatures one of the first persons to be pointed out to a visitor is the Standard Oil lobbyist. Now, no one can dispute the right of the Standard Oil Company to express its opinions on proposed legislation. It has the same right to do this as all the rest of the world. It is only the character of its opposition which is open to criticism, the fact that it is always fighting measures which equalise privileges and which make it more necessary for men to start fair and play fair in doing business.

Of course the effect of directly practising many of their methods is obvious. For example, take the whole system of keeping track of independent business. There are practices required which corrupt every man who has a hand in them.

One of the most deplorable things about it is that most of the work is done by youngsters. The freight clerk who reports the independent oil shipments for a fee of five or ten dollars a month is probably a young man, learning his first lessons in corporate morality. If he happens to sit in Mr. Rockefeller's church on Sundays, through what sort of a haze will he receive the teachings? There is something alarming to those who believe that commerce should be a peaceful pursuit, and who believe that the moral law holds good throughout the entire range of human relations, in knowing that so large a body of young men in this country are consciously or unconsciously growing up with the idea that business is war and that morals have nothing to do with its practice.

And what are we going to do about it? for it is *our* business. We, the people of the United States, and nobody else, must cure whatever is wrong in the industrial situation, typified by this narrative of the growth of the Standard Oil Company. That our first task is to secure free and equal transportation privileges by rail, pipe and waterway is evident. It is not an easy matter. It is one which may require operations which will seem severe; but the whole system of discrimination has been nothing but violence, and those who have profited by it cannot complain if the curing of the evils they have wrought bring hardship in turn on them. At all events, until the transportation matter is settled, and settled right, the monopolistic trust will be with us, a leech on our pockets, a barrier to our free efforts.

As for the ethical side, there is no cure but in an increasing scorn of unfair play — an increasing sense that a thing won by breaking the rules of the game is not worth the winning. When the business man who fights to secure special privileges, to crowd his competitor off the track by other than fair competitive methods, receives the same summary disdainful ostracism by his fellows that the doctor or lawyer who is "unprofessional," the athlete who abuses the rules, receives, we shall have gone a long way toward making commerce a fit pursuit for our young men.

Matthew Josephson: THE ROBBER BARONS

JOHN ROCKEFELLER, who grew up in western New York and later near Cleveland, as one of a struggling family of five children, recalls with satisfaction the excellent practical training he had received and how quickly he put it to use. His childhood seemed to have been darkened by the misdeeds of his father, a wandering vendor of quack medicines who rarely supported his family, and was sometimes a fugitive from the law; yet the son invariably spoke of his parent's instructions with gratitude. He said:

. . . He himself trained me in practical ways. He was engaged in different enterprises; he used to tell me about these things . . . and he taught me the principles and methods of business. . . . I knew what a cord of good solid beech and maple wood was. My father told me to select only solid wood . . . and not to put any limbs in it or any punky wood. That was a good training for me.

But the elder Rockefeller went further than this in his sage instructions, according to John T. Flynn, who attributes to him the statement:

I cheat my boys every chance I get, I want to make 'em sharp. I trade with the boys and skin 'em and I just beat 'em every time I can. I want to make 'em sharp.

If at times the young Rockefeller absorbed a certain shiftiness and trading sharpness from his restless father, it was also true that his father was absent so often and so long as to cast shame and poverty upon his home. Thus he must have been subject far more often to the stern supervision of his mother, whom he has recalled in several stories. His mother would punish him, as he related, with a birch switch to "uphold the standard of the family when it showed a tendency to deteriorate." Once when she found out that she was punishing him for a misdeed at school of which he was innocent, she said, "Never mind, we have started in on this whipping and it will do for the next time." The normal outcome of such disciplinary cruelty would be deception and stealthiness in the boy, as a defense.

But his mother, who reared her children with the rigid piety of an Evangelist, also started him in his first business enterprise. When he was seven years old she encouraged him to raise turkeys, and gave him for this purpose the family's surplus milk curds. There are legends of Rockefeller as a boy stalking a turkey with the most patient stealth in order to seize her eggs.

This harshly disciplined boy, quiet, shy, reserved, serious, received but a few years' poor schooling, and worked for neighboring farmers in all his spare time. His whole youth suggests only abstinence, prudence and the growth of parsimony in his soul. The pennies he earned he would save steadily in a blue bowl that stood on a chest in his room, and accumulated until there was a small heap of gold coins. He would work, by his own account, hoeing potatoes for a neighboring farmer from morning to night for 37 cents a day. At a time when he was still very young he had fifty dollars saved, which upon invitation he one day loaned to the farmer who employed him.

"And as I was saving those little sums," he relates, "I soon learned that I could get as much interest for $50 loaned at seven per cent — then the legal rate of interest — as I could earn by digging potatoes for ten days." Thereafter, he tells us, he resolved that it was better "to let the money be my slave than to be the slave of money."

In Cleveland whither the family removed in 1854, Rockefeller went to the Central High School and studied bookkeeping for a year. This delighted him. Most of the conquering types in the coming order were to be men trained early in life in the calculations of the bookkeeper, Cooke, Huntington, Gould, Henry Frick and especially Rockefeller of whom it was said afterward: "He had the soul of a bookkeeper."

In his first position as bookkeeper to a produce merchant at the Cleveland docks, when he was sixteen, he distinguished himself by his composed orderly habits. Very carefully he examined each item on each bill before he approved it for payment. Out of a salary which began at $15 a month and advanced ultimately to $50 a month, he saved $800 in three years, the lion's share of his total earnings! This was fantastic parsimony.

He spent little money for clothing, though he was always neat; he never went to the theater, had no amusements, and few friends. But he attended his Baptist Church in Cleveland as devoutly as he attended his accounts. And to the cause of the church alone, to its parish fund and mission funds, he demonstrated his only generosity by gifts that were large for him then — first of ten cents, then later of twenty-five cents at a time.

In the young Rockefeller the traits which his mother had bred in him, of piety and the economic virtue — worship of the "lean goddess of Abstinence" — were of one cloth. The pale, bony, small-eyed young Baptist served the Lord and pursued his own business unremittingly. His composed manner, which had a certain languor, hid a feverish calculation, a sleepy strength, cruel, intense, terribly alert.

As a schoolboy John Rockefeller had once announced to a companion, as they walked by a rich man's ample house along their way: "When I grow up I want to be worth $100,000. And I'm going to be too." In almost the same words, Rockefeller in Cleveland, Cooke in Philadelphia, Carnegie in Pittsburgh, or a James Hill in the Northwestern frontier could be found voicing the same hope. And Rockefeller, the bookkeeper, "not slothful in business . . . serving the Lord," as John T. Flynn describes him, watched his chances closely, learned every detail of the produce business which engaged him, until finally in 1858 he made bold to open a business of his own in partnership with a young Englishman named Clark (who was destined to be left far behind). Rockefeller's grimly accumulated savings of $800, in addition to a loan from his father at the usurious rate of 10 per cent, yielded the capital which launched him, and he was soon "gathering gear" quietly. He knew the art of using loan credit to expand his operations. His first bank loan against warehouse receipts gave him a thrill of pleasure. He now bought grain and produce of all kinds in carload lots rather than in small consignments. Prosperous, he said nothing, but began to dress his part, wearing a high silk hat, frock coat and striped trousers like other merchants of the time. His head was handsome, his eyes small, birdlike; on his pale bony cheeks were the proverbial side-whiskers, reddish in color.

At night, in his room, he read the Bible, and retiring had the queer habit of talking to his pillow about his business adventures. In his autobiography he says that "these intimate conversations with myself had a great influence upon my life." He told himself "not to get puffed up with any foolish notions" and never to be deceived about actual conditions. "Look out or you will lose your head — go steady."

He was given to secrecy; he loathed all display. When he married, a few years afterward, he lost not a day from his business. His wife, Laura Spelman, proved an excellent mate. She encouraged his furtiveness, he relates, advising him always to be silent, to say as little as possible. His composure, his self-possession was excessive. Those Clevelanders to whom Miss Ida Tarbell addressed herself in her investigations of Rockefeller, told her that he was a hard man to best in a trade, that he rarely smiled, and almost never laughed, save when he struck a good bargain. Then he might clap his hands with delight, or he might even, if the occasion warranted, throw up his hat, kick his heels and hug his informer. One time he was so overjoyed at a favorable piece of news that he burst out: "I'm bound to be rich! *Bound to be rich!*". . .

In the life of every conquering soul there is a "turning point," a moment when a deep understanding of the self coincides with an equally deep sense of one's immediate mission in the tangible world. For Rockefeller, brooding, secretive, uneasily scenting his fortune, this moment came but a few years after his entrance into the oil trade, and at the age of thirty. He had looked upon the disorganized conditions of the Pennsylvania oil fields, the only source then known, and found them not good: the guerilla fighting of drillers, of refining firms, of rival railroad lines, the mercurial changes in supply and market value — very alarming in 1870 — offended his orderly and methodical spirit. But one could see that petroleum was to be the light of the world. From the source, from the chaotic oil fields where thousands of drillers toiled, the grimy stream of the precious commodity, petroleum, flowed along many diverse channels to narrow into the hands of several hundred refineries, then to issue once more in a continuous stream to consumers throughout the world. Owner with Flagler and Harkness of the largest refining company in the country, Rockefeller had a strongly entrenched position at the narrows of this stream. Now what if the Standard Oil Company should by further steps of organization possess itself wholly of the narrows? In this period of anarchic individual competition, the idea of such a movement of rationalization must have come to Rockefeller forcibly, as it had recently come to others.[1]

[1] The English economist J. A. Hobson has written in this connection: "Each kind of commodity, as it passes through the many processes from the earth to the consumer, may be looked upon as a stream whose channel is broader at some points and narrow at others. Different streams of commodities narrow at different places. Some are narrowest and in fewest hands at the transport stage, others in one of the processes of manufacture, others in the hands of export merchants. . . ." In the case of petroleum the logical "narrows" was at the point of refinery; and inevitably,

Even as early as 1868 the first plan of industrial combination in the shape of the pool had been originated in the Michigan Salt Association. Desiring to correct chaotic market conditions, declaring that "in union there is strength," the salt-producers of Saginaw Bay had banded together to control the output and sale of nearly all the salt in their region, a large part of the vital national supply. Secret agreements had been executed for each year, allotting the sales and fixing the price at almost twice what it had been immediately prior to the appearance of the pool. And though the inevitable greed and self-seeking of the individual salt-producers had tended to weaken the pool, the new economic invention was launched in its infantile form. Rockefeller's partners, Flagler and Harkness, had themselves participated in the historic Michigan Salt Association.

This grand idea of industrial rationalization owed its swift, ruthless, methodical execution no doubt to the firmness of character we sense in Rockefeller, who had the temper of a great, unconscionable military captain, combining audacity with thoroughness and shrewd judgment. His plan seemed to take account of no one's feelings in the matter. Indeed there was something revolutionary in it; it seemed to fly in the face of human liberties and deep-rooted custom and common law. The notorious "South Improvement Company," with its strange charter, ingeniously instrumenting the scheme of combination, was to be un-

raveled amid profound secrecy. By conspiring with the railroads (which also hungered for economic order), it would be terribly armed with the power of the freight rebate which garrotted all opposition systematically. This plan of combination, this unifying conception Rockefeller took as his ruling idea; he breathed life into it, clung to it grimly in the face of the most menacing attacks of legislatures, courts, rival captains, and, at moments, even of rebellious mobs. His view of men and events justified him, and despite many official and innocent denials, he is believed to have said once in confidence, as Flynn relates:

I had our plan clearly in mind. It was right. I knew it as a matter of conscience. It was right between me and my God. If I had to do it tomorrow I would do it again in the same way — do it a hundred times.[2]

The broad purpose was to control and direct the flow of crude petroleum into the hands of a narrowed group of refiners. The refiners would be supported by the combined railroad trunk lines which shipped the oil; while the producers' phase of the stream would be left unorganized — *but with power over their outlet to market* henceforth to be concentrated into the few hands of the refiners. . . .

In John D. Rockefeller, economists and historians have often seen the classic example of the modern monopolist of industry. It is true that he worked with an indomitable will, and a faith in his star à la Napoleon, to organize his in-

Rockefeller and Flagler set in motion their great plan to control the stream. "Just as a number of German barons planted their castles along the banks of the Rhine, in order to tax the commerce between East and West which was obliged to make use of this highway, so it is with these economic 'narrows.' Wherever they are found, monopolies plant themselves in the shape of 'rings,' 'corners,' 'pools,' 'syndicates,' or 'trusts.' " ("The Evolution of Modern Capitalism," p. 142.)

[2] By hearsay the legend has come to me of a private conversation between Mr. Rockefeller and some old friends at dinner long ago in which the oil baron said with emotion. *"I discovered something that made a new world and I did not know it at the time."*

dustry under his own dictatorship. He was moreover a great innovator. Though not the first to attempt the plan of the pool — there were pools even in the time of Cicero — his South Improvement Company was the most impressive instance in history of such an organism. But when others had reached the stage of the pool, he was building the solid framework of a monopoly.

Rockefeller's problems were far more difficult than those for instance of Carnegie, who quickly won special economies through constructing a very costly, well-integrated, technically superior plant upon a favored site. In the oil-refining business, a small still could be thrown up in the '70's for manufacturing kerosene or lubricating oil at a tenth the cost of the Edgar Thomson steel works. The petroleum market was mercurial compared to iron, steel and even coal; there were thousands of petty capitalists competing for advantage in it. Hence the tactics of Rockefeller, the bold architecture of the industrial edifice he reared, have always aroused the liveliest interest, and he himself appeals to us for many reasons as the greatest of the American industrialists. In no small degree this interest is owing to the legend of "Machiavellian" guile and relentlessness which has always clung to this prince of oil.

After the dissolution of the South Improvement Company, Rockefeller and Flagler had come to a conference of the irate diggers of petroleum with mild proposals of peaceful cooperation, under the heading of the "Pittsburgh Plan." The two elements in the trade, those who produced the raw material from the earth and those who refined it, were to combine forces harmoniously. "You misunderstand us," Rockefeller and Flagler said. "Let us see what combination will do."

There was much suspicion. One of Titusville's independent refiners (one of those whom Standard Oil tried to erase from the scene) made a rather warlike speech against the plan, and he recalls that Rockefeller, who had been softly swinging back and forth in a rocking chair, his hands over his face, through the conference, suddenly stopped rocking, lowered his hands and looked straight at his enemy. His glance was fairly terrifying.

You never saw such eyes. He took me all in, saw just how much fight he could expect from me, and then up went his hands and back and forth went his chair. . . .

Where a "deal" across the table could not be effected, Rockefeller might try a variety of methods of expropriation. With his measured spirit, with his organized might, he tested men and things. There were men and women of all sorts who passed under his implacable rod, and their tale, gathered together reverently by Miss Tarbell, has contributed to the legend of the "white devil" who came to rule over American industry.

A certain widow, a Mrs. Backus of Cleveland, who had inherited an oil-refinery, had appealed to Mr. Rockefeller to preserve her, "the mother of fatherless children." And he had promised "with tears in his eyes that he would stand by her." But in the end he offered her only $79,000 for a property which had cost $200,000. The whole story of the defenseless widow and her orphans, the stern command, the confiscation of two-thirds of her property, when it came out made a deep stir and moved many hearts.

In another instance a manufacturer of improved lubricating oils set himself up innocently in Cleveland, and became a client of the Standard Oil for his whole supply of residuum oils. The Rockefeller company encouraged him at first, and sold him 85 barrels a day according to a contract. He prospered for three years, then suddenly when the monopoly was well launched in 1874, his supply was cut down to 12 barrels a day, the price was increased on some pretense, and the shipping cost over the railroads similarly increased. It became impossible to supply his trade. He offered to buy of Rockefeller 5,000 barrels and store it so that he might assure himself of a future supply. This was refused.

"I saw readily what that meant," the man Morehouse related to the Hepburn Committee in 1879. "That meant squeeze you out — Buy out your works. . . . They paid $15,000 for what cost me $41,000. He [Rockefeller] said that he had facilities for freighting and that the coal-oil business belonged to them; and any concern that would start in that business, they had sufficient money to lay aside a fund and wipe them out — these are the words."

In the field of retail distribution, Rockefeller sought to create a great marketing machine delivering directly from the Standard Oil's tank wagons to stores in towns and villages throughout the United States. But in the laudable endeavor to wipe out wasteful wholesalers or middlemen, he would meet with resistance again, as in the producing fields. Where unexpectedly stout resistance from competing marketing agencies was met, the Standard Oil would simply apply harsher weapons. To cut off the supplies of the rebel dealer, the secret aid of the railroads and the espionage of their freight agents would be invoked again and again. A message such as the following would pass between Standard Oil officials:

We are glad to know you are on such good terms with the railroad people that Mr. Clem [handling independent oil] gains nothing by marking his shipments by numbers instead of by names.

Or again:

Wilkerson and Company received car of oil Monday 13th — 70 barrels which we suspect slipped through at the usual fifth class rate — in fact we might say we know it did — paying only $41.50 freight from here. Charges $57.40. Please turn another screw.

The process of "Turning the Screw" has been well described by Henry D. Lloyd. One example is that of a merchant in Nashville, Tennessee, who refused to come to terms and buy from Standard Oil; he first found that all his shipments were reported secretly to the enemy; then by a mysterious coincidence his freight rates on shipments of all kinds were raised 50 per cent, then doubled, even tripled, and he felt himself under fire from all parts of the field. He attempted to move his merchandise by a great roundabout route, using the Baltimore & Ohio and several other connecting roads, but was soon "tracked down," his shipments lost, spoiled. The documents show that the independent oil-dealers' clients were menaced in every way by the Standard Oil marketing agency; it threatened to open competing grocery stores, to sell oats, meat, sugar, coffee at lower prices. "If you do not buy our oil we will start a grocery store and sell goods at cost and put you out of business."

By this means, opponents in the country at large were soon "mopped up"; small refiners and small wholesalers who attempted to exploit a given district were routed at the appearance of the familiar red-and-green tank wagons, which were equal to charging drastically reduced rates for oil in one town, and twice as much in an adjacent town where the nuisance of competition no longer existed. There were, to be sure, embittered protests from the victims, but the marketing methods of Standard Oil were magnificently efficient and centralized; waste and delay were overcome; immense savings were brought directly to the refining monopoly.

But where the Standard Oil could not carry on its expansion by peaceful means, it was ready with violence; its faithful servants knew even how to apply the modern weapon of dynamite.

In Buffalo, the Vacuum Oil Company, one of the "dummy" creatures of the Standard Oil system, became disturbed one day by the advent of a vigorous competitor who built a sizable refinery and located it favorably upon the water front. The offices of Vacuum conducted at first a furtive campaign of intimidation. Then emboldened or more desperate, they approached the chief mechanic of the enemy refinery, holding whispered conferences with him in a rowboat on Lake Erie. He was asked to "do something." He was urged to "go back to Buffalo and construct the machinery so it would bust up . . . or smash up," to fix the pipes and stills "so they cannot make a good oil. . . . And then if you would give them a little scare, they not knowing anything about the business. You know how. . . ." In return the foreman would have a life annuity which he might enjoy in another part of the country.

So in due time a small explosion took place in the independent plant, as Lloyd and Miss Tarbell tell the tale, from the records of the trial held several years later, in 1887. The mechanic, though on the payrolls of the Vacuum Oil Company, led a cursed existence, forever wandering without home or country, until in complete hysteria he returned to make a clean breast of the whole affair. The criminal suit against high officials of the Standard Oil monopoly included Henry Rogers and John Archbold, but the evil was laid by them to the "overenthusiasm" of underlings. Evidence of conspiracy was not found by the court, but heavy damages were awarded to the plaintiff, who thereafter plainly dreaded to re-enter the dangerous business.

These and many other anecdotes, multiplied, varied or even distorted, spread through the Oil Regions of Pennsylvania and elsewhere through the country (as ogre-tales are fed to children), and were accumulated to make a strange picture of Mr. Rockefeller, the baron of oil. Miss Tarbell in her "History," written in her "muckraking" days, has dwelt upon them with love. She has recorded them in rending tones with a heart bleeding for the petty capitalists for whom alone "life ran swift and ruddy and joyous" before the "great villain" arrived, and with his "big hand reached out from nobody knew where to steal their conquest and throttle their future."

But if truth must be told, the smaller capitalists, in the producing field especially, were themselves not lacking in predatory or greedy qualities; as Miss Tarbell herself admits, they were capable of hurrying away from church on Sundays to tap enemy tanks or set fire to their stores of oil. What they lacked, as the Beards have commented, was the discipline to maintain a producers' combination equal in strength to that of the refiners. The other factors in the industry engaged in individualistic marketing or refining ventures were very possibly "mossbacks," as one of the Standard Oil chieftains growled, "left in the lurch by progress."

The campaigns for consolidation, once launched, permitted Rockefeller little rest, and engaged his generalship on many fronts at once. In a curious interview given while he was in Europe, cited by Flynn, he himself exclaimed:

How often I had not an unbroken night's sleep, worrying about how it was all coming out. . . . Work by day and worry by night, week in and week out, month after month. If I had foreseen the future I doubt whether I would have had the courage to go on.

With unblinking vigilance he conducted throughout his company an eternal war against waste. We have spoken of his unequaled efficiency and power of organization. There is a famous note to his barrel factory in his careful bookkeeper's hand which has been cited with amused contempt by his critics, to show how attention to small details absorbed his soul. It reads:

Last month you reported on hand, 1,119 bungs. 10,000 were sent you beginning this month. You have used 9,527 this month. You report 1,092 on hand. What has become of the other 500?

It is not a laughing matter, this affair of 500 barrel bungs, worth at the most a dollar or two in all. Rockefeller's hatred of waste told him that in a large-scale industry the rescued pennies multiplied a million times or more represented enormous potential gains. This was to be true of all the great industrial leaders after Rockefeller's time; the spirit regarded as parsimony is a large-visioned conception of technical efficiency in handling big machines. Thus the feeding of horses, the making of his own glue, hoops, barrels, all was carefully supervised and constantly reduced in cost. Barrels were cut $1.25 apiece, saving $4,000,000 a year, cans were reduced 15 cents, saving $5,000,000 a year, and so forth. In absorbing the services of J. J. Vandergrift, in 1872, Rockefeller had acquired as an ally to his enterprise a combination of small pipe lines called the United Pipe Lines. His lieutenants then constructed more pipes; and by 1876 he controlled almost half the existing pipe lines, some running 80 to 100 miles, to the railroad terminals and shipping points. At this time the largest pipe-line interest in competition with Standard Oil's was the Empire Transportation Company, headed by Colonel Joseph Potts, but dominated by the officers of the Pennsylvania Railroad, which held an option over the entire property.

Himself an aggressive entrepreneur, Potts soon found that he must expand or suffer extinction. To the alarm of the Rockefeller organization, he purchased several big refineries in New York and proceeded to pipe crude oil from the oil fields and over the railroad to the seaboard. Rockefeller vehemently petitioned the railroad to withdraw from his domain. Refused at an interview, he promised that he would take his own measures, and left his adversaries with expressions of sanctimonious regret, the form in which his most deadly threats were usually offered.

It was war, a war of rates. He moved with lightning speed. At once the other railroads, Erie and New York Central, were ordered to stand by, lowering their freight rates for him while he slashed the price of refined oil in every market which Potts reached.

But Potts, a stubborn Presbyterian, fought back harder than anyone Rockefeller had ever encountered. He replied in kind by further price cuts; he then began to build larger refineries at the coast ports, lined up independent oil-producers behind him, and reserves in quantities of tank cars, in barges, ships, dock facilities. During the bitter conflict, with which, as Flynn relates, the hills and fields of Pennsylvania resounded, both sides, and the railroads supporting them as well, suffered heavy wounds. Yet Rockefeller would not desist, since Standard Oil's whole system of organization was endangered.

In the midst of this furious engagement a great blow fell upon the enemies of John D. Rockefeller, as if given by the hand of the God to whom he constantly prayed. During the summer of 1877 the workers of the Baltimore & Ohio Railroad struck against wage cuts and their strike spread quickly to adjacent railroads, raging with especial violence in the Pennsylvania system. The most destructive labor war the nation had ever known was now seen in Baltimore and Pittsburgh, with militant mobs fighting armed troops and setting in flames property of great value in revenge for the many deaths they suffered. During this storm which the railroad barons had sown by cutting wages 20 per cent and doubling the length of freight trains, the Pennsylvania interests quickly came to terms with Standard Oil, so that they might be free to turn and crush the rebellious workers. The entire business of Empire Transportation was sold out to the oil combination at their own terms,

while Potts was called off. In Philadelphia, Rockefeller and his partners, quietly jubilant, received the sword of the weeping Potts.

The oil industry as a whole was impressed with the victory of Standard Oil over a railroad ring which had seemed invincible in the past. In a movement of fear many other interests hastened to make terms with Rockefeller. By the end of 1878 he controlled all the existing pipe-line systems; through a new freight pool he directed traffic or quantities of supplies to the various regions or cities as he pleased.

By 1876 this industry had assumed tremendous proportions. Of the annual output of nearly 10,000,000 barrels, the Standard Oil Company controlled approximately 80 per cent, while exports of petroleum products to the value of $32,000,000 passed through their hands. But in 1877 the great Bradford oil field was opened with a wild boom, the uproarious coal-oil scenes of '59 were enacted anew, crowds rushed to the new fields, acreage values boomed, oil gushed out in an uncontrollable flood — half again as much oil as existed before came forth almost overnight. The markets grew demoralized again, just when Rockefeller seemed to have completed his conquest of the old Oil Regions.

What was he to do? In the two years that followed he directed his organization at the high tension of an ordnance department in wartime, so that piping, refining and marketing capacity might be expanded in time, and the almost untenable supply handled without faltering. With utmost energy a huge building program was carried on and further millions were staked on the hazardous business. Then, holding down the unruly producers, he imposed harsh terms through his pipe lines, refusing storage, forcing them to sell the oil they drilled "for immediate shipment" at the depressed prices of 64 to 69 cents a barrel, or have it run into the ground.

The overproduction could not be stopped. The oil men raged at the great machine which held them in bonds. Once more the independents gathered all their forces together to form a protective combination of their own. They founded the Parliament of Petroleum. They raised funds to construct an immense "free" pipe line running over the mountains to the seaboard, and ridding them at last of the railroads which hemmed them in. The new Tidewater Pipe Line would break Standard's control over railroad rates and bring crude oil to the sea.

Rockefeller's agents now lobbied in the state legislature of Pennsylvania to have the proposed pipe line banned. Failing of this his emissaries were thrown out over the state to buy up right of way in the path of the enemy's advance. But the Tidewater's engineers moved with equal speed and secrecy, eluded the defenses which Rockefeller threw in their way and by April, 1879, completed their difficult project.

From successive stations, the great pumps were to drive oil over the very top of the Alleghenies, and down to Williamsport, touching the Reading Railroad, which had joined forces with the independents. Amid picturesque celebration — while the spies of the Standard Oil looked on incredulously — the valves were opened, the oil ran over the mountain and down toward the sea! Rockefeller was checkmated — but to whom would the producers and their free pipe line sell the crude oil at the seaboard? They had no inkling, though they berated him, of the extent of his control at the outlet.

The opposition to the Rockefeller "conspiracy" now rose to its climax of enthusiasm. The hundreds of petty oil men who fought to remain "independent" and keep their sacred right to flood the market or "hold up" consumers at their own pleasure, won sympathy everywhere; and with the aid of local politicians in New York and Pennsylvania they also had their day in court. Their tumult had grown so violent that at long last the lawmakers of Pennsylvania moved to prosecute the monopolists for "conspiracy in restraint of trade." Writs were served and on April 29, 1879, a local Grand Jury indicted John D. Rockefeller, William Rockefeller, J. A. Bostwick, Henry Flagler, Daniel O'Day, J. J. Vandergrift and other chieftains of Standard Oil for criminal conspiracy, to "secure a monopoly of the oil industry, to oppress other refiners, to injure the carrying trade, to extort unreasonable railroad rates, to fraudulently control prices," etc. Simultaneously in New York State, the legislature appointed a committee of investigation of railroads, headed by the young lawyer A. Barton Hepburn. Forced to look at all the facts which were brought out by the Hepburn Committee, the nation was shocked. The railroad interests, as arch-conspirators, were at once under heavy fire. But no one understood the scope and meaning of the new phase reached in industrial life at this stage, save perhaps Mr. Chauncey Depew, who in a moment of illumination exclaimed on behalf of the railroad interests he so gallantly championed: "Every manufacturer in the state of New York existed by violence and lived by discrimination. . . . By secret rates and by deceiving their competitors as to what their rates were and by evading all laws of trade these manufacturers exist." This was God's truth and certainly true of all the other states in the Union. And of course under the prevailing circumstances there was nothing to be done, save recommend certain "regulative" laws.

With Rockefeller, there had arisen the great industrial combination in colossal and "sinister" form; he was the mighty bourgeois who was to expropriate all the petty bourgeois and his name was to be the rallying cry of parties and uprisings. The outlook for monopoly seemed dark, yet the trial, in the name of a democratic sovereignty which held "sacred" the property of the "conspirators," whatever the means by which they may have pre-empted or confiscated such property — was to be simply a comedy, and was to be enacted again and again. Before the bar of justice, Rockefeller and his brilliant lieutenants would appear, saying, "I refuse to answer on the advice of counsel." A Henry Rogers, a Flagler, would use every shift which such philosophers of the law as Joseph Choate or Samuel C. T. Dodd might counsel. They would "refuse to incriminate themselves" or evade reply on a point of technicality, or lie point-blank. Or, as in the case of the terribly cynical Archbold, they would simply jest, they would make mock of their bewildered prosecutors.

It was Rockefeller who made the most profound impression upon the public. He seemed distinguished in person; with his tall stooping figure, his long well-shaped head, his even jaw. His long, fine nose, his small birdlike eyes set wide apart, with the narrowed lids drooping a little, and the innumerable tiny wrinkles, made up a remarkable physiognomy. But his mouth was a slit, like a shark's. Rockefeller, impeccably dressed and groomed, thoroughly composed, pretendedly anxious to please, foiled his accusers with ease. Every legal subterfuge was used by him with supreme skill. Certain of

his denials were legally truthful, as Flynn points out, since stock-ownership concerning which he was questioned was often entrusted temporarily (in time for such trials) to mere clerks or bookkeepers in his employ.

But the moment came when he was asked specifically about his connection with the notorious refiners' pool of 1872.

"Was there a Southern Improvement Company?"

"I have heard of such a company."

"Were you not in it?"

"I was not."

His hearers were amazed at the apparent perjury he made point-blank with even voice and an inscrutable movement of the eyes. But no! He had been only a director of the *South Improvement Company*, and not of the "Southern Improvement Company," as the prosecutor had named it by mistake.

If Rockefeller was embittered by the cruel fame he won, he never showed it. The silence he preserved toward all reproaches or questions may have been a matter of clever policy; yet it suggested at bottom a supreme contempt for his critics and accusers alike.

"We do not talk much — we saw wood!"

There were times when his movements were hampered, times when he dared not enter the State of Pennsylvania though the authorities there called for him impatiently; times when it was equally convenient to remain almost in hiding at his New York headquarters in Pearl Street, while the world at large howled against him. Yet he moved with unequaled agility and force against all serious attacks upon his industrial barony.

The menace of the Tidewater Pipe Line which cut through his network of railroads and refineries he must crush at all costs. This was far more important than any impeachment of his character. Fertile in expedients at a crisis, he could also be infinitely patient. It used to be said: "To Mr. Rockefeller a day is as a year, and a year as a day. He can wait, but he never gives up." Now when he perceived that the Tidewater's line to the sea was a reality, he besieged it from all sides. On the one hand he offered to buy all the oil it ran, a tempting offer which would have made the affair most profitable to the stockholders. Rebuffed here he proceeded to use the inventions of his rivals and build a long pipe line of his own to the sea. Night and day his engineers and gangs labored in the mountains, to connect the Bradford fields with the Standard Oil terminal at Bayonne. Then before the walls of Bayonne, where lay his great coastal refineries and storage tanks, his pipe line was stopped by an interested railroad from which he would have removed his freight business. The Town Council of Bayonne was induced to be friendly and grant a franchise; the Mayor who resisted for a time was suddenly won over; and in all secrecy, because of the need of haste to prevent a blocking franchise by the railroad, his gangs assembled. There were 300 men ready in the night of September 22, 1879, with all materials, tools, wagons gathered, waiting for the signal — the swift passage of an ordinance by the Town Council and its signing by the Mayor. Then with mad speed the trench across the city was dug, the pipes laid, jointed and covered, before the dawn. The National Transit Company was completed as the largest pipe-line system in the field.

His own line of communications was now secured against the enemy. But he also pursued a campaign of secret stock purchase for control, gaining a minority interest in the Tidewater company, cre-

ating dissensions within, damaging its credit, detaching its officials, instigating suits for receivership, serving writs, injunctions, and more writs, until the managers seemed to struggle for their very sanity. Day by day these blows fell mysteriously, until in 1882 the adversary surrendered and effected the best agreement possible under the circumstances. By this a minor part of the oil-transporting business was apportioned to itself and it yielded up its independence after four years of fighting an unresting, infinitely armed master. All the pipe lines were now amalgamated under Standard Oil control; the great railroads, notably the Pennsylvania, were forced by agreement and in return for a stipulated yearly ransom to retire from the business of oil transportation forever. John D. Rockefeller at the age of forty-four had accomplished his ambition — he was supreme in the oil industry, "the symbol of the American monopolist."

Up to 1881 the forty-odd companies controlled by Rockefeller and his partners formed a kind of *entente cordiale* bound by interchange of stock. This form of union being found inadequate or impermanent, the counsel of the Standard Oil Company, Samuel C. T. Dodd, came forward with his idea of the Trust. By a secret agreement of 1882, all the existing thirty-seven stockholders in the divers enterprises of refining, piping, buying or selling oil conveyed their shares "in trust" to nine Trustees: John and William Rockefeller, O. H. Payne, Charles Pratt, Henry Flagler, John Archbold, W. G. Warden, Jabez Bostwick and Benjamin Brewster. The various stockholders then received "trust certificates" in denominations of $100 in return for the shares they had deposited; while the Trustees, controlling two-thirds of all the shares, became the direct stockholders of all the companies in the system, empowered to serve as directors thereof, holding in their hands final control of all the properties. The Trustees could dissolve any corporations within the system and organize new ones in each state, such as the Standard Oil of New Jersey, or the Standard Oil of New York. Nor could any outsiders or newly arrived stockholders have any voice in the affairs of the various companies. The Trustees formed a kind of supreme council giving a centralized direction to their industry. Such was the first great Trust; thus was evolved the harmonious management of huge aggregations of capital, and the technique for large-scale industry.

Dodd, the resourceful philosopher of monopoly, defended his beautiful legal structure of the "Standard Oil Trust" both in a pamphlet of 1888 and in an argument before a Congressional committee of that year. It was but the outcome of a crying need for centralized control of the oil business, he argued. Out of disastrous conditions had come "cooperation and association among the refiners, resulting eventually in the Standard Oil Trust [which] enabled the refiners so cooperating to reduce the price of petroleum products, and thus benefit the public to a very marked degree." In these arguments, learned economists of the time, such as Professor Hadley, supported Dodd. The Trust, as perfected monopoly, pointed the way to the future organization of all industry, and abolished "ruinous competition."[3]

From their headquarters in the small old-fashioned building at 140 Pearl Street the supreme council of an economic empire sat together in conference like princes of the Roman Church. Here in utmost privacy confidential news brought by agents or informers throughout the world was discussed, and business policies determined. The management and responsibility was skillfully divided among committees: there was a committee on Crude Oil, a committee on Marketing, on Transportation, and numerous other departments. By these new processes markets or developments everywhere in everybody's business were followed or acted upon.

Every day the astute leaders rounded together by Rockefeller lunched together in Pearl Street, and later in a large and famous office building known as 26 Broadway. No one questioned the preeminence of John D. Rockefeller, though Charles Pratt usually sat at the head of the table. The aggressive Archbold was closest to John D. Rockefeller. His brother William Rockefeller, an amiable mediocrity, but immensely rich as well, and long trained in the use of money, depended most upon Henry H. Rogers. Rogers took a more dominant place in the management with the passing years. He is described by Thomas Lawson as "one of the most distinguished-looking men of the time, a great actor, a great fighter, an intriguer, an implacable foe."

These, together with Brewster, Barstow, J. H. Alexander and Bostwick, were the leaders who carried on their industrial operations throughout the world like a band of conspiratorial revolutionists. But "there was not a lazy bone nor a stupid head" in the whole organiza-

---

[3] Dodd explains (in "Combinations," 1888) its origin: "It was a union not of corporations, but of stockholders. . . . From time to time new persons and capital were taken into this association. As the business increased new corporations were formed in various States, some as trading companies, others as manufacturing companies. In some cases the stocks of these companies were placed in the hands of Trustees instead of being distributed to the owners. Out of this grew what is known as the Standard Oil Trust."

tion, as Miss Tarbell has said. Behind them were the active captains, lieutenants, followers and workers, all laboring with the pride, the loyalty, the discipline and the enthusiasm born of the knowledge that "they can do no better for themselves" anywhere than under the "collar" of the Standard Oil. Freed of all moral scruples, curiously informed of everything, they were prompted by a sense of the world's realities which differed strangely from that of the man in the street. They were a major staff engaged in an eternal fight; now they scrapped unprofitable plants, acquiring and locating others; or now they gathered themselves for tremendous mobilizing feats during emergencies in trade. They found ways of effecting enormous economies; and always their profits mounted to grotesque figures: in 1879, on an invested capital of $3,500,000, dividends of $3,150,000 were paid; the value of the congeries of oil companies was then estimated at $55,000,000. Profits were overwhelmingly reinvested in new "capital goods" and with the formation of the Trust capitalization was set at $70,000,000. By 1886 net earnings had risen to $15,000,000 per annum.

"Hide the profits and say nothing!" was the slogan here. To the public prices had been reduced, it was claimed. But after 1875, and more notably after 1881, despite the fluctuations of crude oil a firm tendency set in for the markets of refined oil products. Upon the charts of prices the rugged hills and valleys of oil markets turn into a nearly level plain between 1881 and 1891. Though raw materials declined greatly in value, and volume increased, the margin of profit was consistently controlled by the monopoly; for the services of gathering and transporting oil, the price was not lowered in twenty years, despite the superb

technology possessed by the Standard Oil. Questioned on this, that "frank pirate" Rogers replied, laughing: "*We are not in business for our health, but are out for the dollar.*"

While the policy of the monopoly, as economists have shown, might be for many reasons to avoid *maximum* price levels — such as invited the entrance of competition in the field — it was clearly directed toward keeping the profit margin stable during a rising trend in consumption and falling "curve" in production cost. Similarly in perfecting its technology the Trust was guided by purely pecuniary motives, as Veblen points out, and it remains always a matter of doubt if the mightier industrial combinations improved their service to society at large in the highest possible degree. As often as not it happened that technical improvements were actually long delayed until, after a decade or more, as in the case of Van Syckel's pipe line of 1865, their commercial value was proved beyond a doubt. It was only after rivals, in desperation, contrived the pumping of oil in a two-hundred-mile-long pipe line that Rockefeller followed suit. So it was with the development of various by-products, the introduction of tank cars, etc.

The end in sight was always, as Veblen said, increase of ownership, and of course pecuniary gain rather than technical progress in the shape of improved workmanship or increased service to the community. These latter effects were also obtained. But to a surprising degree they seem accidental by-products of the long-drawn-out struggles, the revolutionary upheavals whence the great industrial coalitions sprang.

The greatest service of the industrial baron to business enterprise seemed to lie elsewhere, as Veblen contended. "The heroic role of the captain of industry is that of a deliverer from an excess of business management." It is a "sweeping retirement of business men as a class from service . . . a casting out of business men by the chief of business men."

John D. Rockefeller said that he wanted in his organization "only the big ones, those who have already proved they can do a big business. As for the others, unfortunately they will have to die."

John D. Rockefeller: SOME EXPERIENCES
IN THE OIL BUSINESS

THE story of the early history of the oil trade is too well known to bear repeating in detail. The cleansing of crude petroleum was a simple and easy process, and at first the profits were very large. Naturally, all sorts of people went into it: the butcher, the baker, and the candlestick-maker began to refine oil, and it was only a short time before more of the finished product was put on the market than could possibly be consumed. The price went down and down until the trade was threatened with ruin. It seemed absolutely necessary to extend the market for oil by exporting to foreign countries, which required a long and most difficult development; and also to greatly improve the processes of refining so that oil could be made and sold cheaply, yet with a profit, and to use as by-products all of the materials which in the less efficient plants were lost or thrown away.

These were the problems which confronted us almost at the outset, and this great depression led to consultations with our neighbors and friends in the business in the effort to bring some order out of what was rapidly becoming a state of chaos. To accomplish all these tasks of enlarging the market and improving the methods of manufacture in a large way was beyond the power or ability of any concern as then constituted. It could only be done, we reasoned, by increasing our capital and availing ourselves of the best talent and experience.

It was with this idea that we proceeded to buy the largest and best refining concerns and centralize the administration of them with a view to securing greater economy and efficiency. The business grew faster than we had anticipated.

This enterprise, conducted by men of application and ability working hard together, soon built up unusual facilities in manufacture, in transportation, in finance, and in extending markets. We had our troubles and set-backs; we suffered from some severe fires; and the supply of crude oil was most uncertain. Our plans were constantly changed by changed conditions. We developed great facilities in an oil centre, erected storage tanks, and connected pipe-lines; then the oil failed and our work was thrown away. At best it was a speculative trade, and I wonder that we managed to pull through so often; but we were gradually learning how to conduct a most difficult business.

Foreign Markets

Several years ago, when asked how our business grew to such large proportions, I explained that our first organization was a partnership and afterward a corporation in Ohio. That was sufficient for a local refining business. But, had we been dependent solely upon local business, we should have failed long since. We were forced to extend our markets into every part of the world. This made the seaboard cities a necessary place of business, and we soon discovered that manufacturing for export could be more economically carried on there; hence refineries were established at Brooklyn, at Bayonne, at Philadelphia, at Baltimore, and necessary corporations were organized in the different states.

We soon discovered, as the business grew, that the primary method of transporting oil in barrels could not last. The package often cost more than the contents, and the forests of the country were not sufficient to supply cheaply the necessary material for an extended time. Hence we devoted attention to other methods of transportation, adopted the pipe-line system, and found capital for pipe-line construction equal to the necessities of the business.

To operate pipe-lines required franchises from the states in which they were located — and consequently corporations in those states — just as railroads running through different states are forced to operate under separate state charters. To perfect the pipe-line system of transportation required many millions of capital. The entire oil business is dependent upon the pipe-line. Without it every well would be less valuable and every market at home and abroad would be more difficult to serve or retain, because of the additional cost to the consumer. The expansion of the whole industry would have been retarded without this method of transportation.

Then the pipe-line system required other improvements, such as tank-cars upon railroads, and finally the tank-

steamer. Capital had to be furnished for them and corporations created to own and operate them.

Every one of the steps taken was necessary if the business was to be properly developed, and only through such successive steps and by a great aggregation of capital is America today enabled to utilize the bounty which its land pours forth, and to furnish the world with light.

The Start of the Standard Oil Company

In the year 1867 the firms of William Rockefeller & Co., Rockefeller & Andrews, Rockefeller & Co., and S. V. Harkness and H. M. Flagler united in forming the firm of Rockefeller, Andrews & Flagler.

The cause leading to the formation of this firm was the desire to unite our skill and capital in order to carry on a business of greater magnitude with economy and efficiency in place of the smaller business that each had heretofore conducted separately. As time went on and the possibilities became apparent, we found further capital to be necessary; then we interested others and organized the Standard Oil Company, with a capital of $1,000,000. Later we saw that more money could be utilized, found persons who were willing to invest with us, and increased our capital to $2,500,000, in 1872, and afterward in 1874 to $3,500,000. As the business grew, and markets were obtained at home and abroad, more persons and capital were added to the business, and new corporate agencies were obtained or organized, the object being always the same — to extend our operations by furnishing the best and cheapest products.

I ascribe the success of the Standard Oil Company to its consistent policy of making the volume of its business large through the merit and cheapness of its products. It has spared no expense in utilizing the best and most efficient method of manufacture. It has sought for the best superintendents and workmen and paid the best wages. It has not hesitated to sacrifice old machinery and old plants for new and better ones. It has placed its manufactories at the points where they could supply markets at the least expense. It has not only sought markets for its principal products, but for all possible by-products, sparing no expense in introducing them to the public in every nook and corner of the world. It has not hesitated to invest millions of dollars in methods for cheapening the gathering and distribution of oils by pipe-lines, special cars, tank-steamers, and tank-wagons. It has erected tank-stations at railroad centres in every part of the country to cheapen the storage and delivery of oil. It has had faith in American oil and has brought together vast sums of money for the purpose of making it what it is, and for holding its market against the competition of Russia and all the countries which are producers of oil and competitors against American products.

The Insurance Plans

Here is an example of one of the ways in which we achieved certain economies and gained real advantage. Fires are always to be reckoned with in oil refining and storage, as we learned by dear experience, but in having our plants distributed all over the country the unit of risk and possible loss was minimized. No one fire could ruin us, and we were able thus to establish a system of insuring ourselves. Our reserve fund which provided for this insurance could not be wiped out all at once, as might be the case with a concern having its plants together or near each other. Then we studied and perfected our organization to prevent fires, improving our appliances and plans year after year until the profit on this insurance feature became a very considerable item in the Standard earnings.

It can easily be seen that this saving in insurance, and minimizing the loss by fire affected the profits, not only in refining, but touched many other associated enterprises: the manufacture of by-products, the tanks and steamers, the pumping-stations, etc.

We devoted ourselves exclusively to the oil business and its products. The company never went into outside ventures, but kept to the enormous task of perfecting its own organization. We educated our men; we trained many of them from boyhood; we strove to keep them loyal by providing them full scope for their ability; they were given opportunities to buy stock, and the company itself helped them to finance their purchases. Not only here in America, but all over the world, our young men were given chances to advance themselves, and the sons of the old partners were welcomed to the councils and responsibilities of the administration. I may say that the company has been in all its history, and I am sure it is at present, a most happy association of busy people.

I have been asked if my advice is not often sought by the present managers. I can say that if it were sought it would be gladly given. But the fact is that since I retired it has been very little required. I am still a large stockholder, indeed I have increased my holdings in the company's stock since I relinquished any part in its management.

Why the Standard Pays Large Dividends

Let me explain what many people, perhaps, fully appreciate, but some, I am sure, do not. The Standard pays four dividends a year: the first in March, which is the result of the busiest season of the whole twelvemonth, because more oil is consumed in winter than at other seasons, and three other dividends later, at about evenly divided periods. Now, these dividends run up to 40 per cent. on the capital stock of $100,000,000, but that does not mean that the profit is 40 per cent. on the capital invested. As a matter of fact, it represents the results of the savings and surplus gained through all the thirty-five or forty years of the workings of the companies. The capital stock could be raised several hundred per cent. without a penny of over-capitalization or "water"; the actual value is there. If this increase had been made, the rate would represent a moderate dividend-paying power of about 6 to 8 per cent.

A Normal Growth

Study for a moment the result of what has been a natural and absolutely normal increase in the value of the company's possessions. Many of the pipe-lines were constructed during a period when costs were about 50 per cent. of what they are now. Great fields of oil lands were purchased as virgin soil, which later yielded an immense output. Quantities of low-grade crude oil which had been bought by the company when it was believed to be of little value, but which the company hoped eventually to utilize, were greatly increased in value by inventions for refining it and for using the residues formerly considered almost worthless. Dock property was secured at low prices and made valuable by buildings and development. Large unimproved tracts of land near the important business centres were acquired. We brought our industries to these places, made the land useful, and increased the value, not only of

our own property, but of the land adjacent to it to many times the original worth. Wherever we have established businesses in this and other countries we have bought largely of property. I remember a case where we paid only $1,000 or so an acre for some rough land to be used for such purposes, and, through the improvements we created, the value has gone up 40 to 50 times as much in 35 or 40 years.

Others have had similar increases in the value of their properties, but have enlarged their capitalization correspondingly. They have escaped the criticism which has been directed against us, who with our old-fashioned and conservative notions have continued without such expansion of capitalization.

There is nothing strange or miraculous in all this; it was all done through this natural law of trade development. It is what the Astors and many other large landholders did.

If a man starts in business with $1,000 capital and gradually increases his property and investment by retaining in his concern much of his earnings, instead of spending them, and thus accumulates values until his investment is, say, $10,000, it would be folly to base the percentage of his actual profits only on the original $1,000 with which he started. Here, again, I think the managers of the Standard should be praised, and not blamed. They have set an example for upbuilding on the most conservative lines, and in a business which has always been, to say the least, hazardous, and to a large degree unavoidably speculative. Yet no one who has relied upon the ownership of this stock to pay a yearly income has been disappointed, and the stock is held by an increasing number of small holders the country over.

The Management of Capital

We never attempted, as I have already said, to sell the Standard Oil stock on the market through the Stock Exchange. In the early days the risks of the business were great, and if the stock had been dealt in on the Exchange its fluctuations would no doubt have been violent. We preferred to have the attention of the owners and administrators of the business directed wholly to the legitimate development of the enterprise rather than to speculation in its shares. The interests of the company have been carefully conserved. We have been criticized for paying large dividends on a capitalization which represents but a small part of the actual property owned by the company. If we had increased the capitalization to bring it up to the real value, and listed the shares on the Exchange, we might have been criticized then for promoting a project to induce the public to invest. As I have indicated, the foundations of the company were so thoroughly established, and its affairs so conservatively managed, that, after the earlier period of struggle to secure adequate capital and in view of the trying experiences through which we then passed, we decided to pursue the policy of relying upon our own resources. Since then we have never been obliged to lean very heavily upon the financial public, but have sought rather to hold ourselves in position not only to protect our own large and important interests, but to be prepared in times of stress to lend a helping hand to others. The company has suffered from the statements of people who, I am convinced, are not familiar with all the facts. As I long ago ceased to have any active part in the management of its affairs perhaps I may venture the opinion that men who devote themselves to building up the sale of American products all over the world, in competition with foreign manufacturers, should be appreciated and encouraged.

There have been so many tales told about the so-called speculations of the Standard Oil Company that I may say a word about that subject. This company is interested only in oil products and such manufacturing affairs as are legitimately connected therewith. It has plants for the making of barrels and tanks; and building pumps for pumping oil; it owns vessels for carrying oil, tank-cars, pipes for transporting oil, etc., etc. — but it is not concerned in speculative interests. The oil business itself is speculative enough, and its successful administration requires a firm hand and a cool head.

The company pays dividends to its stockholders which it earns in carrying on this oil trade. This money the stockholders can and do use as they think fit, but the company is in no way responsible for the disposition that the stockholders make of their dividends. The Standard Oil Company does not own or control "a chain of banks," nor has it any interest directly or indirectly in any bank. Its relations are confined to the functions of ordinary banking, such as other depositors have. It buys and sells its own exchange; and these dealings, extending over many years, have made its bills of exchange acceptable all over the world.

Character the Essential Thing

In speaking of the real beginning of the Standard Oil Company, it should be remembered that it was not so much the consolidation of the firms in which we had a personal interest, but the coming together of the men who had the combined brain power to do the work, which was the actual starting-point. Perhaps it is worth while to emphasize again the fact that it is not merely capital and "plants" and the strictly material things which make up a business, but the character of the men behind these things, their personalities, and their abilities; these are the essentials to be reckoned with.

Late in 1871, we began the purchase of some of the more important of the refinery interests of Cleveland. The conditions were so chaotic and uncertain that most of the refiners were very desirous to get out of the business. We invariably offered those who wanted to sell the option of taking cash or stock in the company. We very much preferred to have them take the stock, because a dollar in those days looked as large as a cart-wheel, but as a matter of business policy we found it desirable to offer them the option, and in most cases they were even precipitate in their choice of the cash. They knew what a dollar would buy, but they were very sceptical in regard to the possibilities of resurrecting the oil business and giving any permanent value to these shares.

These purchases continued over a period of years, during which many of the more important refineries at Cleveland were bought by the Standard Oil Company. Some of the smaller concerns, however, continued in the business for many years, although they had the same opportunity as others to sell. There were always, at other refining points which were regarded as more favourably located than Cleveland, many refineries in successful operation. . . .

All these purchases of refineries were conducted with the utmost fairness and good faith on our part, yet in many quarters the stories of certain of these transactions have been told in such form as to give the impression that the sales were made most unwillingly and only because the sellers were forced to make them by the most ruthless exertion of superior power. . . .

The Question of Rebates

Of all the subjects which seem to have attracted the attention of the public to the affairs of the Standard Oil Company, the matter of rebates from railroads has perhaps been uppermost. The Standard Oil Company of Ohio, of which I was president, did receive rebates from the railroads prior to 1880, but received no advantages for which it did not give full compensation. The reason for rebates was that such was the railroads' method of business. A public rate was made and collected by the railroad companies, but, so far as my knowledge extends, was seldom retained in full; a portion of it was repaid to the shippers as a rebate. By this method the real rate of freight which any shipper paid was not known by his competitors nor by other railroad companies, the amount being a matter of bargain with the carrying company. Each shipper made the best bargain that he could, but whether he was doing better than his competitor was only a matter of conjecture. Much depended upon whether the shipper had the advantage of competition of carriers.

The Standard Oil Company of Ohio, being situated at Cleveland, had the advantage of different carrying lines, as well as of water transportation in the summer; taking advantage of those facilities, it made the best bargains possible for its freights. Other companies sought to do the same. The Standard gave advantages to the railroads for the purpose of reducing the cost of transportation of freight. It offered freights in large quantity, car-loads and train-loads. It furnished loading facilities and discharging facilities at great cost. It provided regular traffic, so that a railroad could conduct its transportation to the best advantage and use its equipment to the full extent of its hauling capacity without waiting for the refiner's convenience. It exempted railroads from liability for fire and carried its own insurance. It provided at its own expense terminal facilities which permitted economies in handling. For these services it obtained contracts for special allowances on freights.

But notwithstanding these special allowances, this traffic from the Standard Oil Company was far more profitable to the railroad companies than the smaller and irregular traffic, which might have paid a higher rate.

To understand the situation which affected the giving and taking of rebates it must be remembered that the railroads were all eager to enlarge their freight traffic. They were competing with the facilities and rates offered by the boats on lake and canal and by the pipe-lines. All these means of transporting oil cut into the business of the railroads, and they were desperately anxious to successfully meet this competition. As I have stated we provided means for loading and unloading cars expeditiously, agreed to furnish a regular fixed number of carloads to transport each day, and arranged with them for all the other things that I have mentioned, the final result being to reduce the cost of transportation for both the railroads and ourselves. All this was following in the natural laws of trade.

Pipe-Lines vs. Railroads

The building of the pipe-lines introduced another formidable competitor to the railroads, but as oil could be transported by pumping through pipes at a much less cost than by hauling in tank-cars in a railroad train the development of the pipe-line was inevitable. The question was simply whether the oil traffic was sufficient in volume to make the investment profitable. When pipe-lines had been built to oil fields where the wells had ceased to yield, as often happened, they were about the most useless property imaginable.

An interesting feature developed through the relations which grew up between the railroads and the pipe-lines. In many cases it was necessary to combine the facilities of both, because the pipes reached only part of the way, and from the place where they ended the railroad carried the oil to its final destination. In some instances a railroad had formerly carried the oil the entire distance upon an agreed rate, but now that this oil was partly pumped by pipe-lines and partly carried by rail, the freight payment was divided between the two. But, as a through rate had been provided, the owners of the pipe-line agreed to remit a part of its charges to the railroad, so we had cases where the Standard paid a rebate to the railroad instead of the reverse — but I do not remember having heard any complaint of this coming from the students of these complicated subjects.

The profits of the Standard Oil Company did not come from advantages given by railroads. The railroads, rather, were the ones who profited by the traffic of the Standard Oil Company, and whatever advantage it received in its constant efforts to reduce rates of freight was only one of the many elements of lessening cost to the consumer which enabled us to increase our volume of business the world over because we could reduce the selling price.

How general was the complicated bargaining for rates can hardly be imagined; everyone got the best rate that he could.

After the passage of the Interstate Commerce Act, it was learned that many small companies which shipped limited quantities had received lower rates than we had been able to secure, notwithstanding the fact that we had made large investments to provide for terminal facilities, regular shipments, and other economies. I well remember a bright man from Boston who had much to say about rebates and drawbacks. He was an old and experienced merchant, and looked after his affairs with a cautious and watchful eye. He feared that some of his competitors were doing better than he in bargaining for rates, and he delivered himself of this conviction:

"I am opposed on principle to the whole system of rebates and drawbacks — unless I am in it."

Allan Nevins: REBATES AND STANDARD OIL

BY 1868 trunk-line competition was spirited, and a battle of giants for both the crude-oil and refined-oil traffic was beginning. The Pennsylvania, already a powerful system, was presided over by J. Edgar Thomson, a shrewd organizer at whose side stood the brilliant vice-president, Thomas A. Scott, who had made so strong a record as Assistant Secretary of War under Lincoln. The New York Central was in the hands of Cornelius Vanderbilt, the dominant railroad genius of the country, who had just completely integrated the lines connecting New York City and Buffalo. He looked forward to an early annexation of the Lake Shore, more than 500 miles in length, as part of a through road from the Atlantic to Chicago.[1] The winter of 1867–68 witnessed the spectacularly shocking "Erie War" between Vanderbilt and the Daniel Drew-Jay Gould forces for control of the Erie Railroad. The latter won, and in the fall of 1868 the unscrupulous Gould was elected president of the Erie. He at once absorbed the Atlantic & Great Western as part of his trunk-line, which thus reached Cleveland.[2] The struggle of these three great systems over the rich quarry of the oil traffic was destined in the next few years to arouse nationwide attention; and it created a situation in which Cleveland and John D. Rockefeller could reach out for high stakes in the refining industry.

The firm of Rockefeller, Andrews & Flagler could obviously ship refined oil east either by the Erie or the Lake Shore-New York Central route, while in summer it could use the waterways. Flagler in 1867 began bargaining. He found that an ambitious young veteran, General James H. Devereux, had just become vice-president and general manager of the Lake Shore Railroad, and was eager to make a record. Devereux hoped to obtain a large oil traffic, for the Lake Shore was just completing its Jamestown & Franklin branch into the very heart of the Oil Regions. Up to this year nearly all crude oil had come into Cleveland by way of the Atlantic & Great Western, but the energetic general meant to change that. Since it was important to be on good terms with the largest refiners, we can imagine him shaking hands eagerly with Flagler.[3]

Unquestionably it was Flagler and not Rockefeller who undertook the negotiations, for late in life he said as much. Speaking of rebates, he remarked: "A lot of rubbish has been printed on that subject, too. Mr. Rockefeller is charged with inventing the plan by which the Standard secretly got advantages over its competitors in the matter of freights.

[1] John Moody, *The Railroad Builders*, pp. 33, 34.

[2] H. S. Mott, *The Story of Erie*, contains a special chapter on the checkered history of the Atlantic & Great Western.

[3] See the affidavit of Devereux in the suit of the Standard Oil Company against Wm. C. Scofield and others in the Court of Common Pleas, Cuyahoga County, Ohio, in 1880, printed in Tarbell, *Standard Oil Company*, I, 277–279.

From *John D. Rockefeller,* Volume I, by Allan Nevins, copyright 1940 by Charles Scribner's Sons. Reprinted by permission of Charles Scribner's Sons.

Now the truth is that I, and not Mr. Rockefeller, was in charge of the transportation department of our business. I remember when the Standard received its first rebate. I went home in great delight. I had won a great victory, I thought. A year later I discovered that other refiners received similar favors."[4] He believed that Tom Scott of the Pennsylvania had introduced rebating, but this is more than dubious.

An agreement on crude-oil shipments was easily reached. Such oil was carried from the Regions to Cleveland at a cent a gallon or 42 cents a barrel. Flagler pointed out that his firm was already much the largest in Cleveland; that its business was invaluable, for it moved both the greatest body of crude oil west and the greatest body of refined oil east; and that both parts of its traffic were growing fast. Rockefeller and he could promise shipments sufficiently large and regular to enable the Lake Shore to effect important economies. As a matter of fact, 42 cents a barrel was excessive. Cleveland was already taking nearly a million barrels of crude oil from the Regions, and in 1870 would take more than two millions; in view of these quantities, rates might well be cut. Undoubtedly other Cleveland refineries had received rebates prior to this time. Rockefeller, like Flagler, has explicitly stated that this was true — that such concessions antedated even his entry into refining.[5] "Rebates and drawbacks were a common practice . . . for many years preceding and many years following this period; that is, the period before 1862 and long after." While this perhaps fixes the practice earlier in petroleum history than it actually occurred, it had become a fairly old story soon after the war.

[4] Interview, N. Y. *Tribune*, Dec. 23, 1906.

[5] Inglis, Conversations with Rockefeller.

In any event, Rockefeller, Andrews & Flagler obtained their rebate in 1867. Though the amount has never been disclosed, it seems to have been not less than fifteen cents a barrel. The Atlantic & Great Western doubtless matched it. Rockefeller records that from this time the New York Central-Lake Shore system and the Erie-Atlantic & Great Western system "regarded us as their allies in the freight-competition."[6] Several years later the head of Alexander, Scofield & Co. told a committee of the Federal House that, rendered suspicious by the prosperity of Rockefeller, Andrews & Flagler, he had gone in 1868 or 1869 to the offices of the Atlantic & Great Western. He said: "You are giving others better rates than you are us. We cannot compete if you do that." The agent did not deny the charge, but offered a compensating rebate. Alexander, Scofield & Co. were to pay the full rate, send in their railroad vouchers every month, and be refunded fifteen cents a barrel on crude oil. W. H. Doane, a shipper of crude oil who served Rockefeller and other refineries, made complaint and obtained a ten-cent rebate — apparently not his first.[7]

It would be interesting to know how many other Cleveland refineries obtained rebates on crude oil, with the precise dates and sums. Probably the smallest shippers got nothing, and paid the published rates. It is also probable that Rockefeller, Andrews & Flagler received a higher allowance than nearly any one

[6] Idem.

[7] Testimony of Messrs. Alexander and Doane, Committee of Commerce of the Federal House of Representatives, April, 1872. Rockefeller, commenting on this, said (Inglis, Conversations) that Alexander was "an ignorant Englishman, with more than the usual amount of conceit," who became jealous. Doane was a good friend of Rockefeller, and his testimony was "not intended at all to be adverse or prejudicial to the Standard Oil Company."

else. According to the code of the time they, with the great power to make demands, would have been foolish had they not exacted it. It was commonly believed in Cleveland that in 1868–70 they also received a rebate on shipments of refined oil, but Flagler, when later examined under oath, declared they had obtained "None whatever." Precise evidence has disappeared along with the railroad books and refinery records. Secrecy was a vital element in rebate-granting. The railroads took care to keep their concessions secret from other roads or other shippers, while the manufacturer held his rates secret from all competitors. "Neither railroad nor shipper," remarks McPherson, "knew what concessions were obtained from other railroads by other shippers." Of course Rockefeller and Flagler had means of guessing at the rebates to other refiners, just as these refiners could guess at the favors accorded to Rockefeller.

But what of the ethics of this special advantage which Rockefeller, Andrews & Flagler had gained? How widespread was the practice of rebating, and how was it regarded by businessmen at the time? Miss Tarbell says that the theory was "generally held then, as now, though not so definitely crystallized into law, that the railroad being a common carrier had no right to discriminate between its patrons."[8] John T. Flynn takes an opposing view. After pointing out that Rockefeller "did not invent the rebate," he states that the principle that the railroad has no right to make discriminatory rates is of more recent birth. "This idea had practically no public support in the sixties. The roads were in the possession of men who believed they had a right to run them to suit themselves. . . . The railroads were in a state of perpetual warfare

[8] Tarbell, *Standard Oil Company*, I, 49.

with each other. The managers were attempting to build their roads and the territory through which they ran. In this competition they made all sorts of concessions to large shippers. And it is quite certain that when Rockefeller and Flagler went to Stone for a rebate they believed they were acting not only within their rights but in accordance with the permissible stratagems of the game."[9]

This is an issue which lies at the very root of any judgment upon Rockefeller's business methods. Elucidation of the subject is also important to an understanding of transportation itself. Curiously enough, neither Miss Tarbell nor Mr. Flynn uses the most authoritative evidence upon the place of rebates in business in 1867–70.

In 1867 the railroad committee of the Ohio Senate made a highly illuminating investigation of railroad rate-practices. Its reports demonstrated that rate-reductions — rebates, drawbacks, special rates — were widely prevalent. Numerous instances of rebating in a variety of industries were cited, and it was shown that the grant of preferences to favored communities, companies, and persons was particularly common in the coal trade. Many railroad officers defended these practices. Though the committee condemned them, it clearly did not know what remedy could be applied. They were the result, it pointed out, of a bitter competition between rival roads, in which the lines "seemed to have been in some measure helpless and in part reckless." These contests were ruinous, being marked by an amount of confusion, trick-

[9] Flynn, *God's Gold*, 137. As Doctor Edwin F. Gay stated to me, rebating was long an almost universal practice in America. It was the child of intense railroad competition and was little known in England only because competition was slight there.

ery, distrust, and empiricism "found in no other branch of business"; but the committee did not know how to reach their root. It condemned fast-freight lines, and recommended that all rate-schedules be published. As a result of the inquiry, a bill was drafted which required publication of charges, forbade all deviation from the open rates, prohibited rebates of any kind, declared railroads to be common carriers, and created a Railroad Commissioner with powers of investigation and enforcement. After passing the Senate, it was defeated in the House. Such legislation was impracticable without concurrent action by neighboring States; for if Ohio forbade special rates and Pennsylvania did not, Ohio railroads and cities would suffer while Pennsylvania railroads and cities gained important advantages.[10]

This inquiry was immediately followed by a similar investigation of the Pennsylvania Senate into "alleged extortionate charges" by the railroads of the Keystone State. Public hearings began May 14, 1867, and after seven sessions in various cities, closed on November 8. Scores of witnesses, whose sworn evidence fills 238 closely printed pages,[11] testified to rate discriminations, rebates, and drawbacks. The inquiry had been provoked by widespread and long-continued public complaint of these evils, which had brought many shippers to the point of desperation. A specimen petition against abuses

by the Pennsylvania Railroad, submitted in 1866, read as follows:[12]

The *special* rates of this company are a discrimination of a more evil character than the regular freight list is. *They are a delusion and a snare.* As, if a man erects works on their line, under the influence of them the company hold him in their inexorable grasp from that moment; as, if he raises his voice or his vote against the company, they can stop his *special* rates, or offer lower rates to his rival in business, and crush him. If the special rates were *legalized,* as we understand it was projected by the company to do, on a sliding scale — (so) that a man shipping one thousand tons should have a low rate, and ten thousand a still lower rate, and one hundred thousand the lowest — we aver that they would be opposed to the principles of a free government that advocates the greatest good to the greatest number; that they would build up a privileged class and would allow no fair and free development of the resources of the State of Pennsylvania.

The witnesses made little complaint that the average level of rates was too high; but they offered universal and frantic complaint that rates were uneven, discriminatory, and shot through with favoritism and privilege. All of the abuses that provoked the Interstate Commerce Act of 1887, the Elkins Act of 1903, and the Hepburn Act of 1906 — that furnished a battleground for defenders and attackers of the railroads during a long generation — appear full-blown in these grievances of the embattled Pennsylvania shippers in 1866–68. Not one is missing. The long-and-short-haul discrimination; the charging of far higher rates at noncompetitive than at competitive points; the semi-secret "special rate" to large shippers; the wholly secret rebate to specially favored shippers; the secret

[10] *Report of Railroad Committee, Ohio Senate Journal,* 1867; see Cleveland *Leader,* Feb. 4, 7, 25, 1867, on the report and bill.

[11] *Testimony before the General Judiciary Committee of the Senate of Pennsylvania Relative to Alleged Extortionate Charges upon the Freight and Passengers by the Railroad Corporations of the Commonwealth* (1868). Hereafter cited as *Pennsylvania Senate Inquiry.*

[12] *Pennsylvania Senate Inquiry,* 7.

drawback, or end-of-the-month refund to a shipper — all are described in detail.

The unfair rate discrimination between different cities need not longer detain us, for they have no application to individual or group rebates and drawbacks. A large miller of Duncannon, Pa., 234 miles east of Pittsburgh on the main Pittsburgh-Philadelphia line, testified that the Pennsylvania Railroad charged him the same sum to haul Western wheat this 234 miles that they charged Philadelphia millers for hauling it 355 miles from Pittsburgh. He then had to pay the regular Duncannon-Philadelphia charge on flour to the latter city. Obviously he could not compete with the Philadelphia mills. Several Pittsburgh oil refiners complained that they suffered by this same discrimination between cities. The Pennsylvania Railroad charged precisely the same amount to haul crude oil from Oil City to Philadelphia, 441 miles, as to haul crude oil from Pittsburgh to Philadelphia, only 355 miles. In other words, the railroad gave Oil City shippers the advantage of free transportation for 86 miles.[13] Nor was this all. Pittsburgh refiners bought their crude oil in the Regions, paying freight down the valley; they refined it in Pittsburgh; and then when they shipped to Philadelphia, they found that the Pennsylvania charged five cents a barrel more on refined oil than on crude, though refined oil was cleaner and less liable to loss by fire! Pittsburgh men also testified that in 1866–67 the Erie and New York Central charged only 45 cents a hundredweight on refined oil from Cleveland to New York, while the Pennsylvania charged 50 cents a hundredweight from Pittsburgh to Philadelphia.[14] In short, Pittsburgh refiners were at a cruel disadvantage in competing with Oil City, Philadelphia, and Cleveland.

But the most important testimony related to various forms of rebates: that is, to "special rates" allowed to rather large groups; to rebates proper, given secretly to individuals at the times they shipped; and to drawbacks, which were secret refunds allowed at the end of the month. Numerous men offered evidence as to the "special rates" granted to large shippers, especially on the Pennsylvania. The Harrisburg freight-agent admitted that in shipments of iron west or east, "all the prominent parties have special rates." He further declared that "as a general thing it [the low rate] is not confined," but that "there may have been instances" where one man alone got it. Moreover, he testified that nobody could find out about the special rates except by inquiry. A shipper living at Port Royal, Pa., gave evidence that special rates were frequent.[15]

The rebate proper, unlike the special rate, was given the individual and not the group. It varied from shipper to shipper, according to his power and his demands. Henry McCormick, a prominent Harrisburg ironmaster, testified frankly to his own acceptance of rebates. He simply could not do business without them, and saw no impropriety in them:[16]

In shipping small quantities along the road, our rates are made to conform to the public toll-sheets. In selling nails or pig-iron in large quantities, we find it impossible to compete with others at toll-sheet rates, to any point at any distance from our works. There don't seem to be any system about it; I have been shipping various articles for ten or twelve years, and the rates seem to be entirely arbitrary, and every man seems to

13 *Ibid.*, 167, 168.
14 *Idem*, 167, 168.
15 *Idem*, 19.
16 *Idem*, 33.

make a special or private bargain with the general freight agent at Philadelphia, Mr. Houston. For instance, I have an inquiry for nails at points in the West or Northwest, and if we were to figure according to the rates given us by the officials of the company, here, it would be entirely out of the question to compete with others. To fix the price of any commodities at points at any distance, we must have a special rate given us by the general agent in Philadelphia; we cannot live by the sheet rates. Those rates seem to be arbitrary.

In short, rate-making on the Pennsylvania and other lines was a chaos. The "special rate" was fairly uniform for large shippers, though each man had to be alert to find out its existence. The individual rebate was not uniform but arbitrary. The drawback was still more secret and capricious. S. K. Hoxsie, a retired builder, pungently described it:[17]

The Pennsylvania company have in their office a very important book which it will be necessary to have examined; it is called in their accounts, drawbacks, and the object of this book is twofold; one object is to favor certain shippers over their road — certain corporations or individuals — and the other is to swell the gross receipts of the road to the satisfaction of the stockholders. The discrimination is much larger than any one, perhaps, outside of their immediate circle, knows anything about. The freight paid by certain parties, for instance, appears to be $7.20 a ton for coal; that is credited, of course, to the gross earnings of the road; that swells up the gross receipts, say for 1866, to $16,717,-289.20; that makes it very satisfactory to the stockholders; it also enables parties whom they wish to favor to keep down competition in coal and lumber. Then that same party goes monthly into the treasurer's office and receives what is called a drawback, secretly — an overcharge, as they term it — the effect [of which] is to satisfy the stockholders on the one side, and prevent competition on the other.

Mr. Hoxsie presented evidence that this drawback system went back at least as far as 1862. The following exchange shows that Rockefeller was doubtless correct in asserting that rebates were well known in oil long before he obtained them in 1867:[18]

Q. — Have you any idea of the percentage of that drawback?
A. — It is impossible to tell; I hold in my hand here from their [the Pennsylvania Railroad's] office, some copies of the drawbacks; they commence at number one, I think, each year, and so run up through the year; I have here number 3865, for the year 1862; on twelve of these drawbacks the company paid out $30,000.

Indeed, we know from other sources that rebating by the anthracite railroads of Pennsylvania had begun at least as early as 1856. In that year the competition between mine-operators in the Schuylkill Valley, operators in the Lackawanna field, and operators in the middle anthracite region, had reached a fierce intensity. These three coal areas were served respectively by the Philadelphia & Reading Railroad, the Delaware, Lackawanna & Western Railroad, and the Lehigh Valley Railroad. Each operating group turned to a supporting railroad for aid. It is recorded that, faced with ruin from the bitter competition of their rivals, the Schuylkill operators in May, 1856, compelled the Philadelphia & Reading officials to grant them a heavy rebate as a means of continuing in business.[19]

The mass of testimony taken by the committee showed that while the Pennsylvania Railroad was the worst offender,

17 *Idem*, 37, 38.

18 *Idem*, 44.
19 Jules I. Bogen, *The Anthracite Railroads: A Study in American Railroad Enterprise*, 50, 51.

all lines carried on similar practices. Various witnesses accused the Lackawanna, the Lehigh Valley, and others, as well as the canal companies. One railroad official said defiantly: "We have special rates for large shippers; if the trade legitimately belongs to us, we charge full rates — that is, if there is no competition for it; if there is competition for it, we give drawbacks."[20]

In short, this report demonstrates that immediately after the war the system of rebates and drawbacks flourished luxuriantly in Pennsylvania, yielding enormous but uneven profits to certain interests, and heavy losses to others. It shows that rebates had been counted in thousands on the Pennsylvania Railroad alone as early as 1862. It indicates that railroads granted and large shippers accepted such rebates as a matter of course; that since rates were arbitrary, with no accepted business code or public authority to govern them, in sheer self-protection everybody had to get the best rate he could. The ironmaster McCormick deplored the situation, saying that he thought it would benefit both railroads and shippers "if a regular tariff were prepared, on equitable principles, over the whole State." Tom Scott and other railroad officers, though full of denials and excuses, likewise evinced a certain queasiness. But nobody indicated any expectation of early reform. Indeed, nobody knew just how reforms could be instituted. The report of the Pennsylvania committee was firm in condemning all rebates. Without heat, it pointed out that although the motives of the railroad managers were doubtless often commendable, all preferences were wrong, and as common carriers the lines had "no right to show partiality among their customers." If any preference were neces-

sary to foster a particular branch of industry, it should be granted by the legislature. But nothing was done to effect any essential modification of law, custom, or corporate practice. The legislature, after disclosing how widespread and indeed general the rate discriminations were, allowed them to continue. As a matter of fact, the fierce competition of the transportation companies in this period of rapid growth made them unescapable, and nobody paid any attention to the Mrs. Partington reproofs of the investigators.[21]

Indeed, in dealing with the long-and-short-haul discrimination, the Pennsylvania committee stated flatly that it was not prepared to recommend legislation "which might result in driving the whole of this through trade out of the State to rival lines." That is, it *was* prepared to approve any rate discriminations which favored Pennsylvania as against New York or Maryland! And meanwhile the same attitude was being taken in other States. Some had statutes which forbade discrimination; some did not. Ohio had various rate laws, one of which, dated back to 1852, forbade any railroad to charge more than three cents a mile for carrying passengers, or five cents a ton-mile for carrying freight over distances of thirty miles or more. Beginning in 1867, it also had a Commissioner of Railroads and Telegraphs to help enforce these laws. But the Commissioner reported in 1870 that strict enforcement would drive some lines into bankruptcy. The maximum-fare law was "entirely disregarded." Of freight charges he remarked: "This is a more fruitful source of complaint than any other subject attempted to be regulated by statute. There

[20] *Pennsylvania Senate Inquiry*, 44.

[21] *Report of the Judiciary Committee of the Senate of Pennsylvania on Extortionate Charges*, 1868, 7 ff.

is not a railroad operated in the State, either under special charter or the general law, upon which the law regulating rates is not, in some way, violated nearly every time a regular passenger, freight, or mixed train passes over it."[22]

The rebate was destined to continue flourishing until the Elkins Act of 1903, effectively enforced by President Theodore Roosevelt, extirpated it.[23] For forty years it was to be a potent and unescapable factor in American business. When Robert M. La Follette became governor of Wisconsin, he had special investigators examine the books of the railroads, and found that they had paid $7,000,000 in rebates between 1897 and 1903 in his State alone.[24] Paul Morton of the Santa Fé Railroad declared in 1903 that there was not a city of a hundred thousand people in the United States in which he could not point to one or more fortunes founded upon railway rebates. From beginning to end these multiform rebates, favoring large shippers as they did, were a powerful ally of consolidation in industry. They were one of the principal factors in promoting the growth of great American cities, and in concentrating industry in these cities in ever larger units.[25]

If rebates existed on the Pennsylvania railroads in 1862–67, we may be sure they existed on the Ohio roads. Indeed, a committee of the United States Senate declared in 1865 of the nation as a whole: "The effect of the prevailing policy of railroad managers is, by an elaborate system of secret special rates, rebates, drawbacks, and concessions, to enrich favorite shippers, and prevent free competition in many lines of trade." It must be remembered that the extremely rapid growth of railways between 1850 and the panic of 1873 had placed their business upon an improvised, hastily arranged, and largely experimental footing. Their managers had to grapple hastily and blindly with complex problems of financing, rate-making, and competition. Only by a process of trial and error could they learn how to regulate charges with some uniformity; and for years the freight toll-sheets had scarcely a speaking acquaintance with logic, consistency, or ethics. The public attitude toward the railroads meanwhile oscillated violently between extremes of love and hate. New and fast-growing communities needed roads so badly that they recklessly issued bonds and made other concessions to obtain them; and down to 1871 the nation itself ladled out far too generous land grants. At the same time, the discontent of the Western farmers with rates which they thought extortionately high was helping to breed the Granger movement. Railroad managers were alternately caressed and assailed, flattered and denounced.[26]

[22] Annual Report, Ohio Commissioner of Railroads and Telegraphs, 1870, pp. 6–8. See the Report of the same commissioner, 1867, p. 23, for a typical instance of rate discrimination, and the justification offered by a railroad official.

[23] Officers of the Erie, New York Central and other railroads tell me that applications for rebates are still frequent, and are met by sending the applicant a brief excerpt from Federal laws on the subject. In 1939 the Pennsylvania Railroad was fined for granting certain rebates.

[24] Ray Stannard Baker, "The Railroads on Trial," McClure's Magazine, Vol. 26 (1926), 13; Congressional Record, XL, 5699 (La Follette's speech), April 23, 1906.

[25] John Burton Phillips, Social and Industrial Effects of Railroad Ratemaking, University of Colorado Studies, III. No. 4.

[26] "The attitude of our public authorities toward the railroads has been very much like that of an injudicious parent toward a wayward child — alternately giving him liberty which he was certain to abuse, and making rules which were so strict that they could not be permanently enforced." A. T. Hadley, "American Railroad Legislation," Harper's Magazine, LXXV (1887), 141 ff.

Most new industries pass through a reckless, disorderly phase; railroading was still new; and most railway managers looked strictly at the day-to-day interests of their roads. They sought in every possible way to build up freight receipts, and when two or more tapped the same territory competition was bitter. "In those days," says McPherson, "there was never enough business to satisfy all of them."[27] Hence they made whatever reductions seemed necessary to gain or hold shippers, and paid commissions to anybody through whose influence traffic could be obtained. Prominent citizens took such commissions; a class of irresponsible agents sprang up who made a living by them. The rigors of competition by rebates, secret rates, sudden cuts, and commission-granting could be moderated only by Federal law or concerted action on the part of railroad heads, and for neither was the time ripe.

As railroads grew in length, rebates increased in importance. In 1869, the New York Central, gaining full control of the Lake Shore, furnished through service to Chicago; in the same year the Pennsylvania acquired the Pittsburgh, Fort Wayne & Chicago, thus offering parallel facilities; the Erie had already reached St. Louis through the Atlantic & Great Western and other connections; and the Baltimore & Ohio was extended to Chicago in 1874. The building up of these great competitive systems lifted rebating from a relatively local to a national status. Its effect upon business became nationwide and revolutionary; and in no field was it to be more revolutionary than in oil.

John D. Rockefeller always intimated that the competitive advantage in his company obtained through rebates was

27 McPherson, *Railroad Freight Rates.*

negligible. "I do not think the Rockefeller firms got better rebates than the others," he said in 1917.[28] He stated that his firm's larger, more regular shipments, with other benefits which their size and efficiency conferred upon the railroads, "should have entitled them to more consideration than the smaller and less regular shippers." He pointed out that "each shipper made the best bargain that he could," and that "it isn't for a moment to be supposed that any intelligent businessman would make shipments without making an effort to get rates — such efforts as he would use, in buying goods, to make the best possible arrangements." But he commented upon the ignorance of every shipper about his comparative standing: "Whether or not he was doing better than his competitor was only a matter of conjecture."

Indeed, Rockefeller repeatedly expressed the belief that small shippers — taking the situation over long periods — obtained as good rebates as any; and that considering the advantages which the large manufacturers offered the roads, "the favored shippers were the small shippers." This was unfounded, as we shall later demonstrate. What we know of the years 1867–70 indicates that Rockefeller, Andrews & Flagler vigorously pushed their opportunities for preferential treatments, and that they secured better rebates than many of their Cleveland competitors for the simple reason that they could bargain with greater power.

But they did have other sources of strength. Rockefeller could justly assert later that his partners and he were better organizers, administrators, and technicians than the other Cleveland refiners. In evidence, he pointed to their careful bookkeeping; to the superior business

28 Inglis, Conversations with Rockefeller.

sagacity which Flagler and he displayed; and to the undisputed primacy of Andrews as a plant-manager. Unquestionably they had ampler and better-planned facilities, commanded greater capital, and operated with more energy and precision than any other refinery in existence. With larger resources and production came increasing opportunities for economy, increasing progress in efficiency. . . .

Few episodes in our business history are more dramatic than . . . [the] appeal of the embattled men of the Oil Regions to the executive and courts of Pennsylvania. . . . [One of its aspects was] a call for suits in the State supreme court to enjoin the Pennsylvania Railroad, the lines of the Erie and New York Central in Pennsylvania, and the Standard Oil against discriminating in favor of any shipper either in freight rates or car distribution. . . . [By the end of 1878] the Attorney-General had filed bills in equity against the Pennsylvania, the Atlantic & Great Western, the Lake Shore, and the United Pipe-Lines, charging an unlawful combination to control the entire oil industry and a refusal to offer proper transportation facilities. He asked for injunctions. . . .[29]

Public hearings on these suits began early in 1879. . . . A. J. Cassatt and other reluctant railroad officers were brought upon the witness stand, as were John D. Archbold, William Frew, Charles Lockhart, J. J. Vandergrift, and others connected with the Standard Oil. B. B. Campbell and his associates recited the Regions' grievances at length. . . . The revelations of the size and power of the Standard combination, of the functions it had assumed as an "evener" of railroad traffic, and of the heavy drawbacks, rebates, and special concessions granted by the railroads, excited astonishment and indignation. . . .

Much of the testimony appeared at length in the press, and all of it was later published as a State document.[30] It is safe to say that many people who knew that rebating was the general rule were staggered by the scope of the favors given to the Standard since the fall of 1877. As we have seen, Cassatt testified that "outside" shippers who sent refined oil from Titusville or Pittsburgh to New York paid $1.44½ a barrel, while the Standard paid only 80 cents. Already *The Railroad Gazette* had expressed a significant opinion. Familiar with the "evener" contracts of 1875 and 1877, its editor remarked that the Standard was collecting roughly fifty cents a barrel on crude-oil shipments for the work and risk of effecting a railroad pool. It had not been expected or intended that the Standard should add this amount to its profits, but that it should cut the price of refined oil and so secure a larger and larger share of the business.[31] This it had done, establishing a very powerful combination. While the railroads cared nothing about promoting a monopoly, they had been helpless to resist the Standard. For some time it had been de-

29 Bradford *Era*, N. Y. *Tribune*, Oct. 8, 1878.

30 *Commonwealth of Pennsylvania vs. The Pennsylvania Railroad, etc.* The suits were brought against each corporation separately.

31 According to the *Annual Cyclopaedia*, 1878, p. 682, the whole body of oil shipments in 1878 amounted to 13,000,000 barrels. The established rate of shipment was $1.50 a barrel, which should have given the railroads $18,500,000 [*sic*]. Actually they received only $5,000,000, the other $13,500,000 being diverted to the Standard Oil. On this statement it is to be noted (1) that the established rates were $1.15 and $1.40, subject to certain discounts to everybody; (2) that the Standard probably paid more than double $5,000,000; and (3) that some of its savings went into the cheapening of refined oil.

livering in New York upon two railroads about 400 carloads of petroleum daily, besides large quantities upon a third; and imagine its power if, in the absence of any contract, it had been free to throw this immense volume of oil at will from one railroad to another! Moreover, the railroads had gladly assented to the arrangement because it was very profitable to them. Before the formulation of this "evening" agreement, "traffic was not secure and rates were a great part of the time unremunerative," while now the roads were making money from oil freights. But, continued *The Railroad Gazette,* in a remarkable pronouncement on the ethics of railroad discrimination —[32]

But in this matter, as in all others, the railroads owe a duty to the community as well as to themselves. And if they at once protect the interests of their stockholders and carry at reasonable rates, they will still be liable to condemnation if they make any unjust discriminations among shippers. And in deciding what is "unjust" in the matter of discriminations, the safety of the community, the freedom of industry, demand that there should be a severe interpretation, and that generally allowances of any kind should be prohibited, which it is not in the power of all in the same kind of business to secure, or which are not in proportion to the cost of the thing or service for which the allowance is made. . . .

But the most unjust of all discriminations are probably those founded on some actual advantage offered by the shipper, for which he secures a disproportionately large allowance. One manufacturer has a siding and loads the cars himself; a competitor carts his goods to the station and leaves them for the company to load. In such a case . . . an allowance may be . . . made so great as to work great injustice against the other shipper. . . . The common carrier should offer all his customers what are practically equal terms — terms which it is possible for them to fulfill. And, we are sure, he will have to do this sooner or later.

Contracts may be made now in practical violation of this principle — in years past we fear that a vast number of such contracts have been made — which yet come within the letter of the law; but we may rest assured that they will not remain within the letter of the law. No community, fully understanding the facts, will permanently endure any such power in carriers or any other organizations as will make it possible at their will to destroy the business of whole classes of people.

This was sound doctrine and, as time proved, sound prophecy. A large number of Eastern newspapers expressed similar opinions. And meanwhile the railroads and Standard Oil were under heavy fire in two other States. In New York the Hepburn Investigation began in the fall of 1878 and furnished the newspapers with sensational material, while in Ohio a legislative inquiry was opened. It proved short-lived, but before it was ended various independent refiners of Ohio had told their stories, and H. M. Flagler had been examined as to the Standard's rebates. The cumulative effect of all this upon public sentiment was great, and the railroads and the Standard Oil realized it. Multitudes became convinced that the Standard Oil Combination, now convicted of exacting a drawback upon other men's shipments of crude oil as well as its own — shipments which in the case of Ohlen alone amounted to about 30,000 barrels during two months of 1878 — was essentially a revival of that South Improvement scheme which had excited such general indignation. The demand for effective railroad regulation was immensely strengthened.

[32] Nov. 1, 1878.

Henry Demarest Lloyd:

THE OLD SELF-INTEREST

THE corn of the coming harvest is growing so fast that, like the farmer standing at night in his fields, we can hear it snap and crackle. We have been fighting fire on the well-worn lines of old-fashioned politics and political economy, regulating corporations, and leaving competition to regulate itself. But the flames of a new economic evolution run around us, and we turn to find that competition has killed competition, that corporations are grown greater than the State and have bred individuals greater than themselves, and that the naked issue of our time is with property becoming master instead of servant, property in many necessaries of life becoming monopoly of the necessaries of life.

We are still, in part, as Emerson says, in the quadruped state. Our industry is a fight of every man for himself. The prize we give the fittest is monopoly of the necessaries of life, and we leave these winners of the powers of life and death to wield them over us by the same "self-interest" with which they took them from us. In all this we see at work a "principle" which will go into the records as one of the historic mistakes of humanity. Institutions stand or fall by their philosophy, and the main doctrine of industry since Adam Smith has been the fallacy that the self-interest of the individual was a sufficient guide to the welfare of the individual and society. Heralded as a final truth of "science" this proves to have been nothing higher than a temporary formula for a passing problem. It was a reflection in words of the policy of the day.

When the Middle Ages landed on the shores of the sixteenth century they broke ranks, and for three hundred years every one has been scurrying about to get what he could. Society was not highly developed enough to organize the exploration and subjugation of worlds of new things and ideas on any broader basis than private enterprise, personal adventure. People had to run away from each other and from the old ideas, nativities, guilds, to seize the prizes of the new sciences, the new land, the new liberties which make modern times. They did not go because the philosophers told them to. The philosophers saw them going and wrote it down in a book, and have believed themselves ever since to be the inventors of the division of labor and the discoverers of a new world of social science. But now we are touching elbows again, and the dream of these picnic centuries that the social can be made secondary to the individual is being chased out of our minds by the hard light of the crisis into which we are waking.

"It is a law of business for each proprietor to pursue his own interest," said the committee of Congress which in 1893 investigated the coal combinations. "There is no hope for any of us, but the weakest must go first," is the golden rule of business.[1] There is no other field of human associations in which any such rule of action is allowed. The man who should apply in his family or his citizenship this "survival of the fittest" theory as it is practically professed and operated in business would be a monster, and would be speedily made extinct, as we do with monsters. To divide the supply of food between himself and his children according to their relative powers of calculation, to follow his conception of his own self-interest in any matter which the self-interest of all has taken charge of, to deal as he thinks best for himself with foreigners with whom his country is at war, would be a short road to the penitentiary or the gallows. In trade men have not yet risen to the level of the family life of the animals. The true law of business is that all must pursue the interest of all. In the law, the highest product of civilization, this has long been a commonplace. The safety of the people is the supreme law. We are in travail to bring industry up to this. Our century of the caprice of the individual as the law-giver of the common toil, to employ or disemploy, to start or stop, to open or close, to compete or combine, has been the disorder of the school while the master slept. The happiness, self-interest, or individuality of the whole is not more sacred than that of each, but it is greater. They are equal in quality, but in quantity they are greater. In the ultimate which the mathematician, the poet, the reformer projects the two will coincide.

Our world, operated by individual motive, is the country of the Chinese fable, in which the inhabitants went on one leg.

[1] Testimony, Trusts, Congress, 1888, p. 215

Yes, but an "enlightened self-interest"? The perfect self-interest of the perfect individual is an admirable conception, but it is still individual, and the world is social. The music of the spheres is not to be played on one string. Nature does nothing individually. All forces are paired like the sexes, and every particle of matter in the universe has to obey every other particle. When the individual has progressed to a perfect self-interest, there will be over against it, acting and reacting with it, a corresponding perfect self-interest of the community. Meanwhile, we who are the creators of society have got the times out of joint, because, less experienced than the Creator of the balanced matter of earth, we have given the precedence to the powers on one side. As gods we are but half-grown. For a hundred years or so our economic theory has been one of industrial government by the self-interest of the individual. Political government by the self-interest of the individual we call anarchy. It is one of the paradoxes of public opinion that the people of America, least tolerant of this theory of anarchy in political government, lead in practising it in industry. Politically, we are civilized; industrially, not yet. Our century, given to this *laissez-faire* — "leave the individual alone; he will do what is best for himself, and what is best for him is best for all" — has done one good: it has put society at the mercy of its own ideals, and has produced an actual anarchy in industry which is horrifying us into a change of doctrines.

We have not been able to see the people for the persons in it. But there is a people, and it is as different from a mere juxtaposition of persons as a globe of glass from the handful of sand out of which it was melted. It is becoming, socially, known to itself, with that self-consciousness which distinguishes the quick from the dead and the unborn. Every community, said Pascal, is a man, and every man, said Plato, is a community. There is a new self-interest — that of the "man called million," as Mazzini named him — and with this social motive the other, which has so long had its own way, has now to reckon. Mankind has gone astray following a truth seen only partially, but coronated as a whole truth. Many civilizations must worship good men as gods and follow the divinity of one and another before civilization sees that these are only single stars in a firmament of humanity. Our civilization has followed the self-interest of the individual to learn that it was but one of the complex forces of self-interest.

The true *laissez-faire* is, let the individual do what the individual can do best, and let the community do what the community can do best. The *laissez-faire* of social self-interest, if true, cannot conflict with the individual self-interest, if true, but it must outrank it always. What we have called "free competition" has not been free, only freer than what went before. The free is still to come. The pressure we feel is notice to prepare for it. Civilization — the process of making men citizens in their relations to each other, by exacting of each that he give to all that which he receives from all — has reached only those forms of common effort which, because most general and most vital, first demanded its harmonizing touch. Men joining in the labors of the family, the mutual sacrifices of the club or the church, in the union of forces for self-defence and for the gains of co-operation on the largest scale in labors of universal concern, like letter-carrying, have come to be so far civilized.

History is condensed in the catchwords of the people. In the phrases of indi-

vidual self-interest which have been the shibboleths of the main activities of our last hundred years were prophesied: the filling up of the Mississippi by the forest-destroying, self-seeking lumber companies of the North; the disintegration of the American family — among the rich by too little poverty, and among the poor by too much; the embezzlement of public highways and public franchises into private property; the devolution of the American merchants and manufacturers into the business dependents — and social and political dependents, therefore — of a few men in each great department of trade, from dry-goods to whiskey; the devolution of the free farmer into a tenant, and of the working-man into a fixture of the locomotive or the factory, forbidden to leave except by permission of his employer or the public; and that melee of injunctions, bayonets, idle men and idle machinery, rich man's fear of poor man and poor man's fear of starvation, we call trade and industry.

Where the self-interest of the individual is allowed to be the rule both of social and personal action, the level of all is forced down to that of the lowest. Business excuses itself for the things it does — cuts in wages, exactions in hours, tricks of competition — on the plea that the merciful are compelled to follow the cruel. "It is pleaded as an excuse by those [common carriers] who desire to obey the [Interstate Commerce] law that self-preservation drives them to violate it because other carriers persist in doing so," says Senator Cullom. When the self-interest of society is made the standard the lowest must rise to the average. The one pulls down, the other up. That men's hearts are bad and that bad men will do bad things has a truth in it. But whatever the general average of morals, the anarchy which gives such individuals their head and leaves them to set the pace for all will produce infinitely worse results than a policy which applies mutual checks and inspirations. Bad kings make bad reigns, but monarchy is bad because it is arbitrary power, and that, whether it be political or industrial, makes even good men bad.

A partial truth universally applied as this of self-interest has been is a universal error. Everything goes to defeat. Highways are used to prevent travel and traffic. Ownership of the means of production is sought in order to "shut down" production, and the means of plenty make famine. All follow self-interest to find that though they have created marvellous wealth it is not theirs. We pledge "our lives, our fortunes, and our sacred honor" to establish the rule of the majority, and end by finding that the minority — a minority in morals, money, and men — are our masters whichever way we turn. We agonize over "economy," but sell all our grain and pork and oil and cotton at exchanges where we pay brokerage on a hundred or a thousand barrels or bushels or bales of wind to get one real one sold. These intolerabilities — sweatshops where model merchants buy and sell the cast-off scarlet-fever skins of the poor, factory and mine where childhood is forbidden to become manhood and manhood is forbidden to die a natural death, mausoleums in which we bury the dead rich, slums in which we bury the living poor, coal pools with their manufacture of artificial winter — all these are the rule of private self-interest arrived at its destination.

A really human life is impossible in our cities, but they cannot be reconstructed under the old self-interest. Chicago was rebuilt wrong after the fire. Able men pointed out the avenues to a wider and better municipal life, but they could not be opened through the private interpositions that blocked the way. The slaughter of railway men coupling cars was shown, in a debate in the United States Senate, to be twice as great as it would be if the men were in active service in war. But under the scramble for private gain our society on its railway side cannot develop the energy to introduce the improved appliances ready to hand which would save these lives, all young and vigorous. The cost of the change would be repaid in 100-per-cent. dividends every year by the money value alone to us of the men now killed and wounded. But we shall have to wait for a nobler arithmetic to give us investments so good as that. The lean kine of self-interest devour the fat kine. The railroad stockholder, idolater of self-interest, lets himself be robbed — like the stockholder of all the railroads in this story — either because he is too rich to mind, too feeble to make himself heard, or too much implicated elsewhere as principal in the same kind of depredation to care or dare to stir what he knows to be a universal scandal. He has become within himself the battle-ground of a troop of warring devils of selfishness; his selfishness as a stockholder clutched at the throat by his selfishness as a parasite, in some "inside deal," feeding on the stockholder; some rebate arrangement, fast-freight line, sleeping-car company, or what not. And, as like as not, upon this one's back is another devil of depredation from some inner ring within a ring. Torn at the vitals, the enlightened swinishness of our *leit-motif* is hastening to throw itself into the sea.

We are very poor. The striking feature of our economic condition is our poverty, not our wealth. We make ourselves "rich" by appropriating the property of others by methods which lessen the total property of all. Spain took such riches from America and grew poor. Modern wealth more and more resembles the winnings of speculators in bread during famine — worse, for to make the money it makes the famine. What we call cheapness shows itself to be unnatural fortunes for a very few, monstrous luxury for them and proportionate deprivation for the people, judges debauched, trustees dishonored, Congress and State legislatures insulted and defied, when not seduced, multitudes of honest men ruined and driven to despair, the common carrier made a mere instrument for the creation of a new baronage, an example set to hundreds of would-be commercial Caesars to repeat this rapine in other industries and call it "business," a process set in operation all over the United States for the progressive extinction of the independence of laboring men, and all business men except the very rich, and their reduction to a state of vassalage to lords or squires in each department of trade and industry. All these — tears, ruin, dishonor, and treason — are the unmarked additions to the "price marked on the goods."

Shall we buy cheap of Captain Kidd, and shut our ears to the agony that rustles in his silks? Shall we believe that Captain Kidd, who kills commerce by the act which enables him to sell at half-price, is a cheapener? Shall we preach and practise doctrines which make the Black Flag the emblem of success on the high seas of human interchange of service, and complain when we see mankind's argosies of hope and plenty shrink into private hoards of treasure, buried in selfish sands to be lost forever, even to cupidity? If this be cheapness, it comes by the grace of the seller, and that is the first shape of dearness, as security in society by the grace of the ruler is the first form of insecurity.

The new wealth now administers estates of fabulous extent from metropolitan bureaus, and all the profits flow to men who know nothing of the real business out of which they are made. Red tape, complication, the hired man, conspiracy have taken the place of the watchful eye of the owner, the old-fashioned hand at the plough that must "hold or drive." We now have Captains of Industry, with a few aids, rearranging from office-chairs this or that industry, by mere contrivances of wit compelling the fruits of the labor of tens of thousands of their fellows, who never saw them, never heard of them, to be every day deposited unwilling and unwitting to their own credit at the bank; setting, as by necromancy, hundreds of properties, large and small, in a score of communities, to flying through invisible ways into their hands; sitting calm through all the hubbub raised in courts, legislatures, and public places, and by dictating letters and whispering words remaining the master magicians of the scene; defying, though private citizens, all the forces and authorities of a whole people; by the mere mastery of compelling brain, without putting hand to anything, opening or closing the earth's treasures of oil or coal or gas or copper or what not; pulling down or putting up great buildings, factories, towns themselves; moving men and their money this way and that; inserting their will as part of the law of life of the people — American, European, and Asiatic — and, against the protest of a whole civilization, making themselves, their methods and principles, its emblematic figures.

Syndicates, by one stroke, get the power of selling dear on one side, and producing cheap on the other. Thus they keep themselves happy, prices high, and the people hungry. What model merchant could ask more? The dream of the king who wished that all his people had but one neck that he might decapitate them at one blow is realized to-day in this industrial garrote. The syndicate has but to turn its screw, and every neck begins to break. Prices paid to such intercepters are not an exchange of service; they are ransom paid by the people for their lives. The ability of the citizen to pay may fluctuate; what he must pay remains fixed, or advances like the rent of the Irish tenant to the absentee landlord until the community interfered. Those who have this power to draw the money from the people — from every railroad station, every street-car, every fireplace, every salt-cellar, every bread-pan, washboard, and coal-scuttle — to their own safes have the further incentive to make this money worth the most possible. By contracting the issue of currency and contracting it again by hoarding it in their banks, safe-deposit vaults, and the government treasury, they can depress the prices of all that belongs to the people. Their own prices are fixed. These are "regular prices," established by price-lists. Given, as a ruling motive, the principles of business — to get the most and give the least; given the legal and economic, physical and mechanical control, possible under our present social arrangements, to the few over the many, and the certain end of all this, if unarrested, unreversed, can be nothing less than a return to chattel slavery. There may be some finer name, but the fact will not be finer. Between our present tolerance and our completed subjection the distance is not so far as that from the equality and simplicity of our Pilgrim Fathers to ourselves. . . .

If our civilization is destroyed, as Macaulay predicted, it will not be by his barbarians from below. Our barbarians come from above. Our great money-makers have sprung in one generation into seats of power kings do not know. The forces and the wealth are new, and have been the opportunity of new men. Without restraints of culture, experience, the pride, or even the inherited caution of class or rank, these men, intoxicated, think they are the wave instead of the float, and that they have created the business which has created them. To them science is but a never-ending répertoire of investments stored up by nature for the syndicates, government but a fountain of franchises, the nations but customers in squads, and a million the unit of a new arithmetic of wealth written for them. They claim a power without control, exercised through forms which make it secret, anonymous, and perpetual. The possibilities of its gratification have been widening before them without interruption since they began, and even at a thousand millions they will feel no satiation and will see no place to stop. They are gluttons of luxury and power, rough, unsocialized, believing that mankind must be kept terrorized. Powers of pity die out of them, because they work through agents and die in their agents, because what they do is not for themselves.

Of gods, friends, learnings, of the uncomprehended civilization they overrun, they ask but one question: How much? What is a good time to sell? What is a good time to buy? The Church and the Capitol, incarnating the sacrifices and triumphs of a procession of martyrs and patriots since the dawn of freedom, are good enough for a money-changer's shop for them, and a market and shambles. Their heathen eyes see in the law and its consecrated officers nothing but an intelligence-office and hired men to help them burglarize the treasures accumulated for thousands of years at the altars of liberty and justice, that they may burn their marbles for the lime of commerce.

By their windfall of new power they have been forced into the position of public enemies. Its new forms make them seem not to be within the jurisdiction of the social restraints which many ages of suffering have taught us to bind about the old powers of man over man. A fury of rule or ruin has always in the history of human affairs been a characteristic of the "strong men" whose fate it is to be in at the death of an expiring principle. The leaders who, two hundred years ago, would have been crazy with conquest, to-day are crazy with competition. To a dying era some man is always born to enfranchise it by revealing it to itself. Men repay such benefactors by turning to rend them. Most unhappy is the fate of him whose destiny it is to lead mankind too far in its own path. Such is the function of these men, such will be their lot, as that of those for whom they are building up these wizard wealths.

Poor thinking means poor doing. In casting about for the cause of our industrial evils, public opinion has successively found it in "competition," "combination," the "corporations," "conspiracies," "trusts." But competition has ended in combination, and our new wealth takes as it chooses the form of corporation or trust, or corporation again, and with every change grows greater and worse. Under these kaleidoscopic masks we begin at last to see progressing to its terminus a steady consolidation, the end of which is one-man power. The conspiracy ends in one, and one cannot conspire with himself. When this solidification of many into one has been reached, we shall be at last face to face with the naked truth that it is not only the form but the fact of arbitrary power, of control without consent, of rule without representation that concerns us.

Business motived by the self-interest of the individual runs into monopoly at every point it touches the social life — land monopoly, transportation monopoly, trade monopoly, political monopoly in all its forms, from contraction of the currency to corruption in office. The society in which in half a lifetime a man without a penny can become a hundred times a millionaire is as over-ripe, industrially, as was, politically, the Rome in which the most popular bully could lift himself from the ranks of the legion on to the throne of the Caesars. Our rising issue is with business. Monopoly is business at the end of its journey. It has got there. The irrepressible conflict is now as distinctly with business as the issue so lately met was with slavery. Slavery went first only because it was the cruder form of business.

Against the principles, and the men embodying them and pushing them to extremes — by which the powers of government, given by all for all, are used as franchises for personal aggrandizement; by which, in the same line, the common toil of all and the common gifts of nature, lands, forces, mines, sites, are turned from service to selfishness, and are made by one and the same stroke to give gluts to a few and impoverishment to the many — we must plan our campaign. The yacht of the millionaire incorporates a million days' labor which might have been given to abolishing the slums, and every day it runs the labor of hundreds of men is withdrawn from the production of helpful things for humanity, and each of us is equally guilty who directs to his own pleasure the labor he should turn to the wants of others. Our fanatic of wealth reverses the rule that serving mankind is the end and wealth an incident, and has made wealth the end and the service an accident, until he can finally justify crime itself if it is a means to the end — wealth — which has come to be the supreme good; and we follow him.

It is an adjudicated fact of the business and social life of America that to receive the profits of crime and cherish the agents who commit it does not disqualify for fellowship in the most "solid" circles — financial, commercial, religious, or social. It illustrates what Ruskin calls the "morbid" character of modern business that the history of its most brilliant episodes must be studied in the vestibules of the penitentiary. The riches of the combinations are the winnings of a policy which, we have seen, has certain constant features. Property to the extent of uncounted millions has been changed from the possession of the many who owned it to the few who hold it:

1. Without the knowledge of the real owners.
2. Without their consent.
3. With no compensation to them for the value taken.
4. By falsehood, often under oath.
5. In violation of the law.

Our civilization is builded on competition, and competition evolves itself crime —to so acute an infatuation has the lunacy of self-interest carried our dominant opinion. We are hurried far beyond the point of not listening to the new conscience which, pioneering in moral exploration, declares that conduct we think right because called "trade" is really lying, stealing, murder. "The definite result," Ruskin preaches, "of all our modern haste to be rich is assuredly and constantly the murder of a certain number of persons by our hands every year." To be unawakened by this new voice is bad enough, but we shut our ears even against the old conscience.

We cannot deal with this unless we cleanse our hearts of all disordering rage. "The rare action is in virtue rather than in vengeance." Our tyrants are our ideals incarnating themselves in men born to command. What these men are we have made them. All governments are representative governments; none of them more so than our government of industry. We go hopelessly astray if we seek the solution of our problems in the belief that our business rulers are worse men in kind than ourselves. Worse in degree; yes. It is a race to the bad, and the winners are the worst. A system in which the prizes go to meanness invariably marches with the meanest men at the head. But if any could be meaner than the meanest it would be they who run and fail and rail.

Every idea finds its especially susceptible souls. These men are our most susceptible souls to the idea of individual self-interest. They have believed implicitly what we have taught, and have been the most faithful in trying to make the talent given them grow into ten talents. They rise superior to our half-hearted social corrections: publicity, private competition, all devices of market-opposition, private litigation, public investigation, legislation, and criminal prosecution — all. Their power is greater to-day than it was yesterday, and will be greater to-morrow. The public does not withhold its favor, but deals with them, protects them, refuses to treat their crimes as it treats those of the poor, and admits them to the highest places. The predominant mood is the more or less concealed regret of the citizens that they have not been able to conceive and execute the same lucky stroke or some other as profitable. The conclusion is irresistible that men so given the lead are the representatives of the real "spirit of the age," and that the protestants against them are not representative of our times — are at the best but intimators of times which may be.

Two social energies have been in conflict, and the energy of reform has so far proved the weaker. We have chartered the self-interest of the individual as the rightful sovereign of conduct; we have taught that the scramble for profit is the best method of administering the riches of earth and the exchange of services. Only those can attack this system who attack its central principle, that strength gives the strong in the market the right to destroy his neighbor. Only as we have denied that right to the strong elsewhere have we made ourselves as civilized as we are. And we cannot make a change as long as our songs, customs, catchwords, and public opinions tell all to do the same thing if they can. Society, in each person of its multitudes, must recognize that the same principles of the interest of all being the rule of all, of the strong serving the weak, of the first being the last — "I am among you as one that serves" — which have given us the home where the weakest is the one surest of his rights and of the fullest service of the strongest, and have given us the republic in which all join their labor that the poorest may be fed, the weakest defended, and all educated and prospered, must be applied where men associate in common toil as wherever they associate. Not until then can the forces be reversed which generate those obnoxious persons — our fittest.

Our system, so fair in its theory and so fertile in its happiness and prosperity in its first century, is now, following the fate of systems, becoming artificial, technical, corrupt; and, as always happens in human institutions, after noon, power is stealing from the many to the few. Believing wealth to be good, the people believed the wealthy to be good. But, again in history, power has intoxicated and hardened its possessors, and Pharaohs are bred in counting-rooms as they were in palaces. Their furniture must be banished to the world-garret, where lie the out-worn trappings of the guilds and slavery and other old lumber of human institutions.

Allan Nevins: A GENERAL EVALUATION

THE story of Rockefeller's life is one of the great romances of American history; but it is not a story which invites swift and easy judgments. For one reason, it is extremely complex; for another, it raises highly debatable economic issues. "Each great industrial trust," writes the English economist Alfred Marshall, in *Industry and Trade*, "has owed its origin to the exceptional business genius of its founders. In some cases the genius was mainly constructive; in others it was largely strategic and incidentally destructive; sometimes even dishonest." He correctly ascribes the Standard Oil Trust to a combination of exceptional constructive ability and astute destructive strategy. The pages of its history — some of them very dark, some brilliantly creditable — show the two elements inextricably mingled. They also show that, as Marshall elsewhere states, "general propositions in regard to either competition or monopoly are full of snares." While some journalists and some politicians will utter sweeping and dogmatic statements upon an industrial aggregation like the Standard Oil, and upon the work of a great business leader like Rockefeller, economists will regard these glib verdicts with distrust. Too many unsolved problems are opened up by such an industrial organization, and too many difficult issues are raised by such an individual career.

Yet on the basis of the facts recorded in these volumes, one judgment may be ventured. It is that the extremes of praise and blame heaped upon Rockefeller were both unwarranted. His enemies during his years of power treated him as one of the arch-criminals of the age. His admirers during his later years of philanthropy lauded him as one of the world's greatest benefactors. Neither estimate possessed historical truth, and neither touched Rockefeller's greatest significance to civilization.

This is not to say that much of the criticism heaped upon Rockefeller and the Standard Oil was not entirely valid. The great combination made a cruel use in its early years, and particularly in 1875–79, of railroad rate discriminations. It practised espionage. It employed bogus independent companies. It used "fighting brands" and local price-slashing to eliminate competitors. Its part in politics was sometimes reprehensible. It paid less attention than it should have done to systematic price-reduction. All this can be set off against its constructive achievements: its elimination of waste and introduction of manifold economies; its application of the Frasch process, the Burton cracking process, and the Van Dyke patents; its standardization of products on a high level of quality; its development of valuable by-products; its ready assistance to other industries, particularly in improving lubricants; its efficiency in home distribution, and its bold vigor in conquering world markets. A fairly heavy indictment can be drawn up to offset the credit items.

But it is clear that for various reasons the indictment was overdrawn. In the first place, because Rockefeller established the earliest of the great trusts a fuller and fiercer light of publicity beat upon it than upon other combinations. The constant investigations and suits placed him and the Standard under a gigantic, pitiless lens. Subsequent combinations were less severely treated. In the second place, the fact that the early investigations took place before the American public realized that combination was an irresistible tendency of the age led to a natural misconception. People thought of the trust as a conspiracy, a dark plot born in greed. Not until later did they see that the formation of trusts, pools, and cartels was a world-wide movement born of industrial conditions and in large part as natural as the upheaval of the tides. In the third place, Rockefeller was singularly unfortunate in some of his enemies, and particularly in the attacks of Henry Demarest Lloyd. Such fabrications as the Widow Backus story, and such distortions as the tale of the Buffalo "explosion," did him a gross injustice, and led to the invention of a totally false stereotype of the man. Finally, Rockefeller was open to harsher attack than most captains of industry because he touched directly the lives of the masses. Carnegie sold his steel to railroads and industries which passed on his charges to an uncomprehending public; Rockefeller sold gasolene and kerosene to every family — and most families were ready to believe the worst whenever oil went up. Altogether, it is not strange that the accusations against Rockefeller and the Standard Oil were very decidedly exaggerated.

It is plain that the place Rockefeller holds in American industrial history is that of a great innovator. He early caught a vision of combination and order in an industry bloated, lawless, and chaotic. Pursuing this vision, he devised a scheme of industrial organization which, magnificent in its symmetry and strength, world-wide in its scope, possessed a striking novelty. The opposition which he met was massive and implacable. Producers, rival manufacturers, courts, legislatures, Presidents, public opinion, fought him at every step. He and his partners marched from investigation to investigation, from suit to suit, under a growing load of opprobrium. But they moved imperturbably forward. They believed that the opposition was mistaken and irrational. In their opinion it represented a wasteful anarchy; the full victory of this competitive *laissez-faire* individualism would mean retrogression, confusion, and general loss. They kept grimly on. The day came when, with Taft in the White House, the government finally won its battle against Rockefeller and the Standard Oil. But by that time intelligent men were comprehending that the struggle against Rockefeller's movement for industrial consolidation was not a struggle against criminality; it was largely a struggle against destiny.

The dominant ideal of pioneering America was one of utter independence and self-sufficiency. Long after the new industrial era was far advanced, men clung to the old faith in a self-balancing system of private ownership, small-unit enterprise, and free competition, and to their belief that this system would give every man a reward roughly proportionate to his industry, integrity, and ability. They were slow to perceive that the industrial system was not self-balancing; that it grew less so decade by decade. They were slow to perceive that men were less and less independent, more and more interdependent. They were reluctant to admit that free competition was steadily becoming more restricted, and that its character was inexorably changing. It was ceasing to be a competition of small businesses and individual firms, and becoming a competition organized by great aggregations. They finally had to confess the truth which Donald Richberg wrote in 1940, and which might have been stated a generation earlier: "Ours is the competition of great collective organizations of capital and labor, the competition of huge corporations and large labor organizations. It is the competition of industries with other industries, the competition of overpowering advertising and propaganda." Nor was it altered merely in the scope of the units involved. It was for various reasons no longer a *free* competition in the sense in which it had been free in 1860, or 1880.

Rockefeller was a realist; one of those realists who, as Pareto teaches, have a better grasp of realities than the intellectuals who operate with theories and ideals. Partly by intuition, partly by hard thought, he divined the real nature of economic forces, and the real motives operative in American industry. He and the other leaders of the "heroic age" in American business development thus constituted the guiding elite, in a modern sense, of our industrial society. Many of the forces and elements in that society were irrational and wasteful; Rockefeller wished to impose a more rational and efficient pattern, answering to his own intuitions and deductions. Behind this desire he placed an intellectual keenness, a skill in organization, and a dynamic personal force which were not surpassed, and possibly not equalled, by those of any other industrial captain in history. He was not a product of economic determinism, for he rose superior to it; but he wished to give the economic world a

form in which determinism would meet fewer obstacles. He expressed the full potentialities of a movement which shattered the old industrial order, and he naturally incurred the hostility of the masses.

Rockefeller's economic vision, and the courage shown in his fidelity to it, deserve commendation. He knew that he was carrying through a great experiment, and he believed the experiment sound and fruitful. As our national history lengthens and we gain a truer perspective, the importance of this experiment becomes clearer. It is true that some of his methods were open to criticism; but then it must be remembered that he had to use the weapons and implements of his time. Few books are more needed, in the study of our past, than a thorough examination of the development of business ethics in America. Such standards are progressive, and the steps by which they have improved from generation to generation constitute a fascinating topic. Henry Lee Higginson once told a Harvard class that when he entered the banking and brokerage business, men accepted as perfectly correct practices which the best firms a generation later sharply condemned. In 1870, when a rich customer placed a heavy order for stocks, the broker felt it proper to order a few hundred shares on his own account and thus profit from the rise. By 1900 good brokers condemned such an act. By 1940 it would have been punished by very severe penalties. In talking with Samuel Harper, Rockefeller once remarked that his trust had committed acts in the seventies and eighties which advancing business standards had later made clearly improper. When the history of our business ethics is written, it will doubtless be found that some correlation exists between boom periods and business laxity, between depression periods and an advance in morals. It will also be found that business honesty is correlated with social maturity. An old, long-settled, and fairly static community has better standards than an adolescent, fast-changing district; an old industry has higher ethics than a new industry. All this must be remembered in appraising Rockefeller's weapons and the use he made of them.

The question of motive enters into any consideration either of economic vision or of business ethics; and it is important because some writers of the muckraking school have grievously misconstrued the motives not only of Rockefeller but of a whole generation of business leaders. They sum up these motives in the word "greed," as if it were greed which led Carnegie to build steel mills, Rockefeller to organize the oil industry, Westinghouse to develop the electrical industry, and Ford to manufacture motor cars. If we wish to misuse the word greed we can apply it in many contexts. We can say that Shakespeare was greedy for fame, Lincoln greedy for political power, and Duse greedy for applause. But such a word means nothing in the analysis of motive. What these figures were really interested in was competitive achievement, self-expression, and the imposition of their wills on a given environment. And these were precisely the motives which actuated Carnegie, Westinghouse, and Rockefeller. We have quoted early in this biography a statement by Rockefeller that "achievement" was his great aim, and the statement was true. The word greed may seem apposite to industrial leaders because they accumulated large fortunes. But any careful analysis of the work of the best leaders shows that money was not the central object, but a by-product. Greedy men exist, but they seldom accumulate colossal fortunes,

for greed tends to defeat itself in complex business operations. The corner grocer may be greedy, the political boss, the literary hack. But greed usually stops with the few hundred thousand dollars that purchase satiety. The men who built the really towering economic structures were not thinking primarily of dollars, or they would have halted at the first story.

And one great fact to be borne in mind when studying Rockefeller and his fellow-captains of industry is pointed out by Van Wyck Brooks in *America's Coming of Age*. It is the fact that American business has typically been a more optimistic, light-hearted venture than in other lands, and the best businessmen have been great adventurers. The giants of the "heroic age" of industry can aptly be compared with the famous Elizabethan captains — with Drake, Hawkins, Cavendish, Frobisher, Cabot (some of whom were canny businessmen too). In business, as I have pointed out, Americans of the nineteenth century found the Great Game. They played it with zest and gusto, they enjoyed it even when it was perilous, and they took its ups and downs with equanimity. As Herbert Spencer said in 1882, for Americans it was the modern equivalent of war. If it was hard-hitting and ruthless, so is war; and even when the blows were hardest, it remained a game. "Business in America," wrote Brooks, "is not merely more engaging than elsewhere, it is even perhaps the most engaging activity in American life." Of all its leaders, none showed more boldness or swiftness than Rockefeller, and none more equanimity in accepting defeats and victories. Love of the game was one of his motives, particularly as his keen eye saw a pattern in the game that less discerning men missed.

We have said that his place in the history of business was that of a great innovator; and that is also his place in the history of philanthropy. This man who remolded one industry and offered a design for remaking others crowned his activities by the colossal grant of some $550,000,000 to various objects. But the unexampled scale of his gifts is not their most striking feature. What made his donations arresting and memorable was in larger part the skill with which he planned and organized them. From the beginning his gifts were made thoughtfully and conscientiously. The huge foundations which he, his son, and their aides set up, governed by able men working in greater and greater independence, have become models for large-scale philanthropy in this and other lands. Their aims, administrative mechanism, methods, and not least of all, their spirit, offer lessons which have been widely copied. Foundations had existed long before — but never any quite like these. His emphasis upon ameliorative work at the fountainheads of evil, upon the use of money to stimulate men to self-help, and upon the establishment of *continuing* activities, has been of the highest value.

A correct appraisal of his role as philanthropist will avoid the excessive praise which many have given him because of the sheer amount of his benefactions. The size of his fortune, as we have said, was a historical accident. There was obviously no true sense in which he had earned his billion dollars,[1] any more than Carnegie had earned his half-billion. Only the special economic, legal, and fiscal situation in the United States between 1865 and 1914 made such huge accumulations possible. Rockefeller always recognized this fact, and always regarded himself as

a trustee rather than an owner. His statement at the University of Chicago that "God gave me the money" is sometimes quoted as an arrogant utterance; like Napoleon's statement in putting on the iron crown of Lombardy, "God has given it to me — let man touch it at his peril"; like George F. Baer's statement that God had given the anthracite business to a picked group of men. Actually Rockefeller made that statement in a spirit of utter humility. He devoutly believed that God had made him a trustee for these hundreds of millions, not to be kept but to be given wisely and carefully. And it is for the wisdom, the conscientious effort, and the vision which he and his son lent to the task of distribution — a laborious and difficult task — that gratitude is really due them. The animating generosity, too, is to be counted to his credit. For we must not forget that Rockefeller began to give as soon as he began to earn.

It is earnestly to be hoped that no such fortune will ever again pass into a single grasp. The American people have determined that such aggregations of wealth are incompatible with the best interests of the land. And yet it would be a bold critic who would say that this fortune was an unhappy accident. It passed into the hands of a man who had proved the possession of certain strong liberal impulses. As an ill-clad youth earning a few dollars a week, his own necessities poorly met, he had given a substantial part of his meager wage to charity. Few indeed are those who make such sacrifices for altruistic objects as are recorded in Ledger A. He had given from the outset without regard to religion or race, to Catholic and to Negro. He kept on giving more and more as his income grew. The fortune went to a man who had also proved a remarkable capacity for plan-

---

[1] The word "billion" is here used in a general sense; Rockefeller never possessed that much at a time, though much more than that sum passed through his hands.

82

ning and organizing; who knew how to call expert and farsighted assistants to his side; and who was so devoid of egotism that, having once given funds to agents whom he trusted, he cut himself off from all further control over the money. The United States has in one form or another wasted a great many billions of its wealth. Indeed, waste is a conspicuous part of our national life. It was perhaps a happy accident that a single billion passed into the temporary control of a man who, with his son and his expert counsellors, tried to show how much of public welfare and advancement could be purchased by its careful use.

The life of Rockefeller, we can say again, is not one which invites swift and dogmatic judgments. The lessons which men draw from it will vary according to the preconceptions with which they approach the subject. Some will give a heavier weight to the debit items in the ledger than others. But it can safely be said that the prime significance of Rockefeller's career lies in the fact that he was a bold innovator in both industry and philanthropy; that he brought to the first a great unifying idea, which he insisted should be thoroughly tested, and to the second a stronger, more expert, and more enduring type of organization. It can be said also that by virtue of his organizing genius, his tenacity of purpose, his keenness of mind, and his firmness of character, he looms up as one of the most impressive figures of the century which his lifetime spanned. His fame went around the world, and it will be long before the world forgets it.

Lewis Galantière:

JOHN D.: AN ACADEMY PORTRAIT

TRADE could not be managed by those who do manage it," Dr. Johnson said comfortably, "if it presented much difficulty." Still, provided that you don't stop to quarrel about the adjective, it is easy to demonstrate that Mr. Rockefeller was a great man. Draw up two lists of prominent Americans — one of men who lived before the Civil War, the other of men active after the Civil War. You will find that your first list is made up of men engaged in politics, your second of men engaged in business. In the second list, the name of Rockefeller stands easily first, easily ahead of such names as Morgan, Carnegie, Vanderbilt, Hill, Pullman, Huntington and the rest. Except for Cleveland (and in another era Wilson), what men of politics were of the stature of these business men? Not Fish, not Hay; and certainly none of the servants of business — Depew, Choate, Elihu Root.

Many things explain the differences between the two lists; but the broadest explanation is perhaps that before the Civil War the most exciting thing that talent could do on this continent was to govern the people, while after the Civil War it was to exploit the resources of the continent. The characteristic of our own time — post-1932 — is perhaps that the wheel has swung full circle. A few years ago the President was reported as saying to Mr. Grace of the Bethlehem Steel Corporation, "No one will ever make a million dollars a year again in America." Beginning in 1933, we saw the young graduates of the law schools pour not into the downtown law factories but into the government bureaus. Some years ago Jim Wadsworth and Hamilton Fish were the only St. Mark's boys in the Congress: today politics is striated with the colors of the old school ties. Partly, this is due to the coming of bigness, the divorce of ownership from management, with its inculcation of the attitude of quasi-civil-service in the "young executives" stratum. Everybody (so to say) works for something immeasurably higher than any individual: the biggest and now the least hampered of these work-providing anonymities is government; talent will go increasingly into government as government moves increasingly toward the supervision and even direction of the uses to which the labor and savings of the nation shall be put. No world could be farther from resurrectibility than Mr. Rockefeller's.

Standard Oil in Mr. Rockefeller's day was in many ways the prototype of great American enterprise. It was by no means our first incorporated company; it was not even the first attempt at monopoly; but its founder was very likely the first American enterpriser to carry over into

This review of Allan Nevins's *John D. Rockefeller* is reprinted from the *New Republic*, December 9, 1940, pp. 795–797, by permission of the editors.

the domain of big business the Puritan's horror of waste and detestation of gambling — which waste and gambling were paradoxically the chief traits of nineteenth-century America. Another Standard Oil quality, again reflecting its head, was remoteness from shortsighted greed. Mr. Rockefeller could discriminate between the pennies to be clutched and those not to be clutched. His product was the best: this monopolist always produced as if he had competitors. He never failed to distinguish between the economies that could be effected by superior management and the false savings that brought losses through stoppage of production, desertion by underpaid officials, rejection by the market of inferior goods. Mr. Nevins tells us that his wage policies were always generous, and that is very likely. Unlike the farm-boys and horse-traders who ran great American enterprise seventy years ago, he encouraged his department heads to train others to work while they "sat down, cocked up their heels, and thought out some way for the Standard Oil to make money." Mr. Nevins does not say so, but from a remark dropped by Flagler in this book I am ready to believe that the Standard Oil people had much to do with the invention of that most baffling and fascinating department of business, corporate accountancy. All these were innovations and were among the reasons for its strength.

Most business men of Mr. Rockefeller's time were lucky, luckier even than they were greedy, wasteful and ruthless. Europe was sending us *gratis* a flow of immigrants whom it had brought to maturity of muscle, if not always of mind, at immense expense to itself. They had to be fed, clothed, sheltered, which is to say, they constituted a ready market as well as labor power. Every raw material

needful to them was here, virtually free for the enterpriser's taking. A man had to be a blubbering idiot not to make money in America after the Civil War: he had to be crazy or an habitual gambler to lose it. Most of Mr. Rockefeller's contemporaries in business were gamblers; a great many were fools; and of both Mr. Rockefeller took the fullest advantage. All, meanwhile, were handicapped as against him by the fact of being men: they had desires, weaknesses, passions. Mr. Rockefeller had the immense advantage of being a calculating machine — or as Mr. Nevins calls him, a man with the intellect of a chess player. "I have never had a craving for anything," Mr. Rockefeller said once; and this ghastly declaration, which Christ would have been too humble, Socrates too wise, and Calvin not arrogant enough to utter, seems to have been true. Except an irascible temper, to which he himself refers but of which Mr. Nevins gives no example, the great man had no weakness: there was nothing in this being that demanded self-discipline. In his quiet, secret, self-deprecatory way he was perhaps the most remarkable subject for psychological scrutiny ever thrown up on this continent.

Mr. Nevins, who is no psychologist, deals with his hero from the outside. He shows that he grew up in the skirts of the mother he so much resembled in temperament and appearance; that as a child he bought candy by the pound and sold it to his family by the piece; that as an adolescent he had already earned, saved and lent to a neighbor $50 at seven percent, thus discovering the self-generative power of capital; that his father ("a master of business precept," says Mr. Nevins admiringly) taught his son the tricks and dodges of business by a method which the teacher himself — a cancer quack and money lender — explained in these words: "I cheat my boys every time I get the chance. I want to make 'em sharp. I trade with my boys and skin 'em and I just beat 'em every time I can. I want to make 'em sharp." (For those who like the story of the Jew who stepped aside as his child jumped from a height in order to teach the child to trust not even his father, the training of Rockefeller *père* will seem uncommonly Hebraic.) Mr. Nevins shows his hero mature at every point before his twentieth year, already a donor to charity, and at twenty-one a trustee of his church.

Less importance is lent by the author to Mr. Rockefeller's religion than in my view it merits. It had quite other effects than merely to offer "this unemotional youth an outlet" and instruct him in charity. This peculiar Christianity, which is concerned with the here and not the hereafter, which is respectful of conduct and indifferent to the notion of an immortal soul, which confuses the conception of sin (essentially self-defilement) with a cautious regard for the criminal code (injury to others, not to self), explains a great deal of Mr. Rockefeller's career, no less than character. Mr. Rockefeller once told a Bible class that a customer had threatened to leave his commission firm unless Mr. Rockefeller advanced funds to him before the presentation of the bills of lading covering the goods against which the money was to be loaned. Our hero refused; the customer "flared up angrily," but he continued to do business with Clark and Rockefeller. "I have ever since believed," Mr. Rockefeller said, "that he originated the suggestion to tempt us to do what we stated we did not do, as a test." This, I have no doubt, was profoundly Mr. Rockefeller's notion of temptation to sin; it was his idea of the essence of Chris-

tianity. His solemn conviction that what he practised was religion, and not merely business ethics, his belief that the purely temporal precepts by which he lived constituted eternal spiritual doctrine, had the immense significance of persuading him that all his acts were, if not inspired by God, at any rate approved by God. Mr. Nevins says that he never failed in anything: it is more significant that he never believed himself wrong in anything (and I do not mean merely acknowledged himself wrong, for I am persuaded that he was not a hypocrite). Thus, of his part in the scandalous South Improvement Company he said in later years: "I had our plan clearly in mind. It was right. I knew it as a matter of conscience. It was right between me and my God."

Mr. Nevins, resolved above all to be fair to a man long and often maligned, is led by this sort of thing into the paths of pointlessness and illogic. In the instance of the South company he absolves his hero by a remarkable example of the *ignoratio elenchi:* since Mr. Rockefeller discussed the scheme fully in letters to his wife, Mr. Nevins concludes that "this goes far to prove that he was convinced he was following a proper course, for Mrs. Rockefeller was a highly religious woman with stern moral standards." But as Mr. Rockefeller himself was, by Mr. Nevins' showing, highly religious and sternly moral, the appeal to his wife's standards is certainly supererogatory. Further, Mr. Rockefeller's conviction is not at issue: the question is whether he did or did not participate in the wrongdoing which the author imputes to his associates. (This question Mr. Nevins answers by making his hero guilty of a "great error" of judgment in aligning himself "with an arrangement so repugnant to public sentiment.") Finally, the letters displaying the innocence of heart in which Mr. Rockefeller "kept her fully informed" are not reproduced; though space is taken for his expressions of self-justification.

The story which Mr. Nevins has to tell is in the main sordid and not, as one might think the tale of a great accomplishment should be, exhilarating, or tragic. The individual producers of crude petroleum were as shortsighted and greedy as gold prospectors, and were besides, dependent for their success upon the transport companies. The independent refiners were greedy, too. As the required investment in refining was small, and the prices paid by the public were high (Mr. Nevins is vague about the consumer aspect), there was always big money to be made in the industry. The railroads struggled for the oil traffic ruinously until Mr. Rockefeller showed them how to settle their differences; but in such a way that when the roads had helped him to put his competitors out of business (or into his business), they found themselves his victims, since he could swing a tremendous volume of traffic from road to road. They had, therefore, to recoup themselves, as to millions of dollars annually, by excessive rates on other goods.

The classic Standard Oil schemes were: (1) to get a lower shipping rate than rivals paid, and to get in addition, in cash from the roads, the difference between the two rates paid by the competitors; (2) to choke off crude supplies from competitors; (3) to force the transport companies to deny the competing refiners access to markets; (4) to work the fifth-column game by bribing servants of rival companies, putting their own people into those companies, or secretly buying up a competitor and obtaining the trade secrets of rival groups

through the officials of the company secretly acquired. This is, of course, far from the whole story. The other side of the picture involves the general position of the economy and the technological advances in industry — both of which in a sense drove industrial combines into being — and the superior gifts of the Standard Oil management. But though Mr. Nevins makes a great deal of the fact that vision and efficiency yielded the Standard Oil crowd great profits, he nowhere attributes any important part of those profits to the more reprehensible methods by which Standard Oil obtained its monopoly; and his attitude to Mr. Rockefeller reminds one of the story of Jake Shubert protesting indignantly: "What! *I* should use Shubert methods?" Mr. Rockefeller was never ruthless, to say nothing of anything more unpleasant — "just very acquisitive," says his biographer.

The truth is, Mr. Nevins possesses no point of view except the resolve to be fair, and no acquaintance with political economy such as would permit him to make out the case for industrial combines in general, and Standard Oil in particular, which can legitimately be made. Possessing no affirmative philosophy, he is unable to dominate his subject, but writes surrounded by the horizonless timber of his endless materials. Innocent of economics, he is unable to relate the general to the particular, except by the reiteration of moral judgments which are of no value. He is loyal to his materials, and much more scrupulous in setting forth each separate instance of unfair practice than he need have been; but what he gives with his right hand he takes away with his left, for as only separate instances are examined, as the method of "on-the-one-hand and on-the-other-hand" is employed, he never gets anywhere. He does not deal with his subject in respect of the economy as a whole, or discuss the public interest except as one large abstraction or another is brought out in the records of public hearings which form part of the source material he was bound to examine. He is so little a political scientist that he strikes a parallel between the acts of an individual and the acts of a sovereign government, comparing, *on the grounds of propriety,* the Rockfeller procedure with the AAA. He is so innocent of financial practice that he praises Mr. Rockefeller as one who never watered his stock — quite ignoring the fact that stocks are watered to be sold to the public, whereas up to the time of Mr. Rockefeller's retirement, the stock of Standard Oil was owned exclusively by its founders and their partners or heirs.

Every reader of this work must feel that Mr. Nevins is throughout on the defensive, determined to be fair, not to let his temperamentally liberal bias appear. It is this which, in my view, has led him into the vain moralizing and the excessive concern with detail which mar what might have been a reasonably complete and detached history of an important phenomenon. Only an economic historian could defend the defensible aspect of the Standard Oil combine: for a good part of the task which he set himself Mr. Nevins, the political historian, was not adequately equipped.

Chester McA. Destler: WEALTH AGAINST COMMONWEALTH, 1894 AND 1944

THE closing years of the nineteenth century brought the American people as a nation consciously face to face with problems of which it had been uneasily aware since the Civil War. In the decade before the Spanish-American War left us fumbling toward a new orientation in world affairs, two outstanding books had surveyed the domestic scene and probed searchingly the nation's political and economic structure. Both authors, one an Englishman and the other an American with an even more penetrating mind, were friends and defenders of the best they found and fearless critics of the weaknesses they discovered. Both writers lifted national thought above the pettiness of contemporary squabbles over tariffs, pensions, free silver, and the tag ends of Reconstruction and focused attention on basic political and economic issues that were never again obscured.

The Englishman was James Bryce, whose *American Commonwealth* appeared in 1888. With objectivity and disarming friendliness he measured our institutions and political mores. Where other foreign critics had infuriated, Bryce won a hearing because we felt that at heart he was one with us in our hopes, and we heard willingly the warnings that seemed but echoes of our own unexpressed fears. Amid all the pages of praise and blame there was one pas-

sage that fell on the sensitive ear like an alarm bell in the night. A few sentences selected from this forecast of things to come are an appropriate introduction to the work of his American contemporary:

There is a part of the Atlantic where the westward speeding steam-vessel always expects to encounter fogs. On the fourth or fifth day of the voyage, while still in bright sunlight, one sees at a distance a long low dark-gray line across the bows, and is told this is the first of the fog-banks which have to be traversed. Presently the vessel is upon the cloud and rushes into its chilling embrace, not knowing what perils of icebergs may be shrouded within the encompassing gloom. So, America, in her swift onward progress, sees, looming on the horizon and now no longer distant, a time of mists and shadows, wherein dangers may lie concealed whose form and magnitude she can scarcely yet conjecture. . . . In fact the chronic evils and problems of old societies and crowded countries, such as we see them in Europe, will have reappeared on this new soil. . . . It will be the time of trial for democratic institutions.

Although near the close of this passage Bryce suggests that the time of reckoning lies "not more than thirty years ahead," he goes on to predict that the next few years "or even decades" will be preoccupied with popular attempts to regulate and curtail the powers of the

Reprinted from the *American Historical Review*, 50 (October, 1944), 49–69, by permission of the editors and the author. The original article amplifies the argument in footnotes, here omitted.

great corporations with even more strenuous attacks upon the "Trusts." In 1894, six years after the publication of the *American Commonwealth,* there appeared a volume entitled *Wealth against Commonwealth.* In incisive and vigorous prose, English exposition at its best, the American author Henry Demarest Lloyd marshaled the scholarship of many years to show that the time was here and now to challenge the misuse of accumulated wealth and to break the grip of certain great corporations like Standard Oil upon the economic life of the nation. Lloyd, a man economically well-advantaged himself, was preaching no formulated socialistic doctrine. He was challenging corporate power and wealth and irresponsibility in the name of the commonmonwealth of democratic institutions. His work, which well merits mention in the same bracket with Bryce, was acclaimed in its day and echoed in the literature of the next decade. What Lloyd treated fully and cited by book and candle, the muckrakers publicized in fields he did not cultivate. Those Lloyd pilloried were the originals of Theodore Roosevelt's "malefactors of great wealth." The pat phrases of later writers rattled off the armor of great corporations, but Lloyd's spear had found the weak spots and from his thrusts, weighted with scholarship, they have never freed themselves. The attack upon Lloyd and *Wealth against Commonwealth* comes in cycles. It is sharpest when, as in recent years, the papers of some of the capitalists of an earlier day are opened by families to the use of historians writing official and definitive biographies. All of them, especially those who deal with the Standard Oil coterie, must reckon with Lloyd and each has. In the name of Lloyd and of historical accuracy I propose to deal with some of these critics

in as impersonal a manner as a long interest in Lloyd permits.

It may be well, however, to recall the main facts about the author of *Wealth against Commonwealth.* There can be no doubt of his fitness to undertake a study of the Standard Oil and the trusts. Trained in the law and the rules of evidence under Francis Lieber and Theodore W. Dwight in the Columbia Law School, he had acquired in subsequent years an extraordinary theoretical and technical equipment for such a task. After a thorough grounding in the theories of orthodox economics he had abandoned them, after serious study, for the historical school. This was before Richard T. Ely returned from Germany to introduce the historical approach into academic circles. He was equally familiar with the philosophical and religious movements of the period, especially with Social Darwinism and the "gospel of wealth." While assistant secretary of the American Free Trade League he had learned the importance of exhaustive, meticulous research to which was attributable much of his success throughout a distinguished journalistic career. Seven years as financial, real estate, and railroad editor of the then independent and liberal Chicago *Daily Tribune* had given him an almost unequaled firsthand knowledge of business practices and railroad management at a time when the Standard Oil was perfecting its alliance with the railroads and completing its monopoly. He had employed this in making the first sustained, penetrating, and comprehensive study of corporate and speculative capitalism in America, in the course of which he paid full attention to the petroleum monopoly. Published during the course of a decade (1874-85) in the *Tribune,* the *Atlantic Monthly,* and the *North American Re-*

view, his findings established his reputation as a leading American authority on the combination movement, market manipulations, and railroad management.

During the same period Lloyd worked for a higher standard of business ethics. He fought for public control of the railroads, discovered the labor movement, and dedicated his life to economic reform. Searching for principles that could serve as the foundation for such a program, he turned to Emerson, the philosophy and ethics of Thomas Davidson and Mazzini, the Ethical Culture movement, and Christian and Fabian Socialism. From them he distilled an ethical theory and an ideal of human brotherhood broad enough to include the working class, whose elevation must be a major object of "The New Conscience." In fact, Lloyd came to regard economic problems as fundamentally ethical in character, and the labor movement as an ethical revolt that would overthrow classical economics, democratize labor relations, and monopolistic exploitation of the masses, and vitalize the churches with a truly social gospel. To further these ends, he vainly sought the collaboration of others in the preparation of a factual, carefully documented "Bad Wealth Series." These books were to reveal with infallible accuracy the brutal, unethical methods by which great fortunes and the control of American economic life were being concentrated in the hands of ruthless monopolists. They were intended also to expose the fatal consequences of this process for free enterprise in business, for labor, for democracy itself. Lloyd believed that when presented with these facts the American people would abandon the success fantasy and pioneer in a new democracy based on brotherhood, a finer social

ethics, and social control of the great corporations.

Wealth against Commonwealth was the second volume in the "Bad Wealth Series," a fact that establishes its true character beyond dispute. Although it took the trust movement as its subject, it was not a formal economic treatise or simple economic history. Its first object was to make a realistic study of the pathological aspects of corporate capitalism. Furthermore, Lloyd intended to employ the results of his analysis in a formidable attack upon Social Darwinism and laissez faire economics. His ultimate purpose was to secure a hearing for a new social philosophy that should supply the theoretical basis for effective democratic action in opposition to prevailing economic trends. On the one hand, he was preoccupied with the monopoly movement as an emerging system of power. On the other, he hoped to stimulate the development of a more than countervailing democratic power which, once in the ascendancy, would harmonize and subordinate large scale economic organization to the ideals of freedom, equality, and humanity in the great society. Such purposes elevate the book from a mere muckraking tract, as some have supposed it to be, to a social document of high potentiality.

They explain, also, the peculiar organization and style of presentation that distinguish the book. With the objects that he had in view it was possible for Lloyd to concentrate on the main action, to pay but limited attention to the historical setting, and to ignore chronological sequence when convenient. His discussion of the trusts, of their methods and policies, of the Standard Oil as their prototype and initiator, was presented therefore in a series of dramatic episodes replete with piercing epigrams, employing antithesis in telling fashion to heighten contrasts that in turn are pointed up by striking summaries. It disregarded or took for granted the normal, legitimate aspects of competitive business and focused attention upon the methods that had produced the trusts. "Bad wealth" rather than good was the subject because, as Socrates had said to Callicles, "the greatest are usually the bad, for they have the power."

Upon the truth of his narrative and the correctness of his conclusions rested Lloyd's hope of gaining acceptance of his system of social thought. He did his utmost, therefore, to place his factual frame of reference beyond controversy so that public attention might not be distracted from the main issues. Regarding sworn testimony, adjudicated issues, and official reports as the most reliable of all data, he based his book upon the proceedings of courts, Interstate Commerce Commission, and official investigations wherever possible. These were supplemented by use of the daily press, by counsel with such noted investigators as Simon Sterne and James T. Hudson, by information drawn firsthand from participants in the struggle against monopoly. Cognizant of the fact that the oil trust destroyed its records and guarded its secrets with almost terrifying taciturnity, Lloyd drew upon the sworn testimony of its managers, official apologies published by S. C. T. Dodd, newspaper interviews of John D. Rockefeller, and such unofficial Standard Oil organs as the Oil City *Derrick*. In describing litigation he almost invariably followed the evidence that won the case, although not neglecting to state the side of the defense. Before going to press he compared his quotations and accounts of litigation with the official records and listened to the criticism of lawyers familiar with each important case. So far as its factual framework is concerned, therefore, the presumption is that *Wealth against Commonwealth* makes a faithful, accurate presentation of available data. Heavily documented, it was long regarded as a work of painstaking accuracy.

Scholarly interest in *Wealth against Commonwealth* has increased ever since Charles and Mary Beard associated its shattering effect upon American complacency with the milder shock administered previously by the *American Commonwealth*. Although a noted student of Populism dismissed Lloyd's work as a "famous tract" the tendency among historians was for some time to emphasize its historical accuracy. In a single year, the authors of three outstanding books vied with each other not only in paying tribute to Lloyd's influence but also in emphasizing the reliability of his account of the development of the Standard Oil monopoly. To John Chamberlain, it was a "daring and first-rate" "book of facts . . . bolstered by all future investigation." John T. Flynn's widely read work on John D. Rockefeller termed Lloyd's narrative "thoroughly faithful and authentic," "a specific, an able, a serious, and a disinterested indictment" whose publication rendered a "historic service," while more than one passage in *God's Gold* corroborated Lloyd's earlier findings. Finally, the Pulitzer Prize winning biography of Grover Cleveland, published by Allan Nevins, described *Wealth against Commonwealth* as "a searching exposure, amply buttressed by detail" and paid tribute to the accuracy with which it described "the iniquities of the trusts," the history and "sordid record of business piracy" of the Standard Oil, all of which "was laid bare in more than five hundred calm, unemotional pages." "Nothing," Nevins declared, "escaped Lloyd's keen eye."

The verdict of these scholars on the accuracy of *Wealth against Commonwealth* would, in all probability, have remained unchallenged had not the last of them reversed his earlier judgment. After wide investigation, in which he had been given access to the private papers of John D. Rockefeller, Allan Nevins published a biography of the great oil magnate that painted his portrait in softer, more friendly colors than had previously been exhibited and that stressed the constructive achievements of the Standard Oil. In this work, Professor Nevins asserts that the excessively harsh popular indictment of both must be attributed "particularly" to "the attacks of Henry Demarest Lloyd." Then, after tilting repeatedly in his own narrative against *Wealth against Commonwealth*, Nevins subjects it to a withering attack. As "industrial history" he declares it to be "almost utterly worthless," not to be trusted "at any point," prejudiced, one-sided, omitting the case for the Standard Oil, even dishonest. Lloyd, Nevins charges, was an incompetent investigator, a rhetorical and hysterical journalist without "high literary gifts," dishonest though admittedly earnest and sincere. So detailed and sweeping is this indictment that if it stands *Wealth against Commonwealth* must be regarded as an unfounded polemic, its author classed with William Lloyd Garrison.

To scholars interested in the career and influence of Henry Demarest Lloyd the contradiction between this last evaluation of his book and the earlier estimates of his reliability raised a historical

problem of first importance. So fundamental were the issues involved that until the conflict was resolved no reappraisal of Lloyd's character and career was possible. Upon the final adjudication of the question, also, depended the survival of the now almost traditional story of the rise of the Standard Oil and its contemporary monopolies, a story that originated with Lloyd's disclosures, or the acceptance of the narrative offered in *John D. Rockefeller, The Heroic Age of American Enterprise*.

When this work appeared a rather random checking of footnote references to *Wealth against Commonwealth* uncovered some startling discrepancies between its contents and Nevins' account of them. Discovery of five or six instances of this character, and of Lloyd's superior accuracy when one controversial point was referred to the sources used by both authors, cast some doubt on the validity of the sweeping attack that had been made on both Lloyd and his book. This led to a careful investigation, the object of which was to test the truth of the numerous counts in Mr. Nevins' indictment. Lloyd's qualifications, his motives in writing, the purpose and character of the book, the accuracy of its narrative when checked carefully against its sources, and the degree to which its findings were accepted by competent, contemporary scholars have all been considered. Lloyd's publications and private papers, and primary and secondary historical materials related to the petroleum industry and the trusts have been examined. An entirely independent investigation was made of the Toledo "gas war" of 1887–99 in order to evaluate the account contained in *Wealth against Commonwealth*. To make sure that the Standard Oil viewpoint was not overlooked, permission was sought and secured to make use of parts of the manuscript "John D. Rockefeller's Conversations with William O. Inglis" for this appraisal, subject to no restriction other than a promise of fairness and of making an accurate description of it in the text. These "conversations" were a major source cited by Mr. Nevins in his biography. They were dictated by the elder Rockefeller after his seventy-ninth birthday (1917–18) as he listened to the reading of passages from *Wealth against Commonwealth* and Ida Tarbell's *History*. Although the oil magnate was not conducting a debate with either author, his lengthy statements contain as full a reply to the charges made by them against him and the Standard Oil as he was then able or willing to make. Their significance is increased by the fact that they were intended for his son rather than for publication. On the other hand, they were dictated without reference to documents or other primary sources. The manuscript, therefore, must be classed in the field of reminiscences, subject to the customary reservations in regard to reliability in treating incidents that had occurred from thirty to fifty years before. It should be observed, furthermore, that the story told here of the origin and development of the Standard Oil is similar in theme and character to that related by the great oil monopolist, after careful coaching by his lawyers, on the witness stand in November, 1908, and to the short volume of published reminiscences that appeared in the following year. All or parts of the "Conversations" that bear upon chapters VI to X, XII to XIII, XXII to XXVI, and XXIX to XXXV of *Wealth against Commonwealth* have been used in this appraisal. Excerpts from the missing sections of the manuscript, however, have been found in Nevins' *Rockefeller*.

This investigation has established beyond hope of effective denial that *Wealth against Commonwealth* was the product of six years of patient, exhaustive, and remarkably farflung investigation and research. The sources drawn upon and Lloyd's careful verification of the narrative create a presumption that the book makes a faithful, reliable presentation of the facts. To test the validity of this presumption an extensive verification was undertaken of its footnotes, undocumented statements, and quotations. Of the 648 footnotes citing source materials in the book, 420 have been checked against the sources. In 410 of the 420 notes traced, the sources bear out the statements of the text. In ten only, none of great import, do the citations fail to support the narrative. In addition, 241 unsupported statements were traced back to the sources. Of these 229 were completely verified, eight partially so, only four were actually incorrect. Here again the mistakes modify the narrative only to a slight degree. Scores of quotations checked in like manner were found to be accurate to an unusual extent. Since the book has been called one-sided by defenders of the Standard Oil viewpoint it should be observed that of the 649 footnotes and unsupported statements verified, at least 170 of them came from spokesmen and officials of the oil monopoly, while at least thirty more were made by railroad officials friendly to it. Many of these present the side of the Standard Oil although others, it should be observed, were admissions that Lloyd incorporated in his indictment of the oil combination.

When attention is turned to specific chapters and episodes in the book, verification yields positive results to a surprising degree. The account of the anthracite coal monopoly (chapter II) stands supported by subsequent investigations. The criminal activities of the whiskey trust depicted in chapter III are fully supported by the sources, the description of its evolution verified by comparison with contemporary scholarship. The account of the beef trust (chapter IV) reproduces accurately the report of the Senate investigating committee of 1893 and stands unreversed by subsequent revelations. The lengthy account of the activities of the Standard Oil, though supplemented now in great detail by later scholarship, has been verified to an extent that is amazing in light of the sweeping criticisms of Allan Nevins. Three chapters (XV–XVII) that describe the attempt of George Rice, Marietta, Ohio, refiner, to compete with the oil monopoly in the South and West are astonishingly restrained in the use they make of damaging admissions on the witness stand by the Standard Oil's wholesale distributor for the South and by railroad officials in league with him. The five chapters that describe the Toledo "gas war" of 1887–94 have been substantiated in very large measure by the independent investigation alluded to above, a study that drew upon all pertinent material including sections of the "Inglis Conversations." Its findings have been published in the *Quarterly Bulletin of the Historical Society of Northwestern Ohio*, April, 1943, and may be compared with *Wealth against Commonwealth* at leisure. A most careful examination of the sources cited (chapter XIII) has verified almost line for line Lloyd's description of the collusion between John D. Archbold of Standard Oil and the attorney general of Pennsylvania in a tax suit, and Archbold's bribery of Elisha G.

Patterson into betrayal of the petroleum producers while still under contract to the state in the same tax suit. The account of Standard Oil's shabby treatment of Samuel van Syckel, inventor of the process of continuous distillation as well as builder of the first successful petroleum pipe line, has also been verified adequately. Neither Mr. Nevins nor Rockefeller's "Conversations with Inglis" disputes the facts in chapter VI, which describes how the Standard Oil used rebates secured from the Lake Shore and Michigan Southern Railroad to force Scofield, Shurmer, and Teagle of Cleveland into an admittedly illegal refiners' pool in 1876. Lloyd's account of the South Improvement Company and how it was used by the Standard Oil to gain control of the refining industry in Cleveland, his description of the building of the Tidewater Pipe Line, the struggle between it and the railroad-Standard Oil combination, and the latter's final triumph, his story of the rate war between the Pennsylvania and the northern trunk lines in 1877 that forced the former to sell the Empire Transportation Company to the Standard Oil, all stand the test of verification. So does the account of how the oil monopoly employed its own long-distance pipe lines to throttle the railroads and use them in maintaining the monopoly that it had just established with their assistance. Equally well established is the account of the railroad rate and service discriminations imposed in the eighties in the interest of Standard Oil, of the great producers' shutdown of 1887–88, of the ruthless means employed by the oil combination in stamping out competition. Miss Tarbell, John T. Flynn, and Mr. Nevins add details that fill out the narrative and alter from time to time the interpretation of men and motives. But when all allowances are made,

Lloyd's pioneering report on the methods by which the oil monopoly was established and maintained remains substantially unaltered, although later authorities emphasize more the role of economy and efficiency in the rise of the Standard Oil. Lloyd's condemnation of the South Improvement scheme; the account of the refineries of the Oil Region dismantled by the oil combination; the description of the heavy concentration of its capital investments in pipe lines, of the widespread espionage directed at competitors, of the decisive role of freight-rate favors in competition between refining companies, of the brutal coercion of competitors when they resisted amicable persuasion to sell out or enter the combination, of the use of bogus independent companies, and of destructive local price-cutting, and to a limited extent the assertion that the Standard Oil marketed inferior products, were all corroborated by Nevins' *Rockefeller*.

Some of the more important cases of alleged inaccuracy in *Wealth against Commonwealth* must now be considered. On the highly controversial issue of whether the South Improvement Company ever did any business, Lloyd's well-supported assertion that it did is true under a fair definition of the phrase. Lloyd did not assert that the Standard Oil Company was simply the South Improvement Company resurrected. But he did establish beyond dispute a significant continuity between the two in personnel. Further continuity was shown in the repeated application of the idea of forcing a monopoly upon the refining industry by means of alliance with the railroads. As applied by the Standard Oil this entailed not only exceptional rate and service favors but also on several occasions drawbacks on rates paid by competitors, use of the pooling device as

a means to ultimate absorption of competitors, railroad assistance in espionage, and rates on oil shipments from Cleveland and Pittsburgh to the seaboard equal to or lower than those given the Oil Region, to the ruin of the refining industry of the latter.

In dealing with Standard Oil's development Lloyd's zeal in discovering its misdeeds led him occasionally to overlook or minimize evidence that would have modified his narrative. This is true of his brief treatment of the "immediate shipment" controversy of 1879. Here he fails to note that the basic problem was the lack of tankage for storage purposes that was precipitated by the tremendous increase in production of the Bradford field. This situation the Standard Oil was doing its utmost to meet by building additional tankage. Lloyd's chivalrous attitude toward women and his distrust of John D. Rockefeller as the "gentleman pirate" of the oil industry led him to do the oil magnate less than justice in describing the purchase of the Backus Oil Company of Cleveland by the Standard Oil in 1878. The original affidavits used in the preparation of this account have long since disappeared from the archives of the Cuyahoga county clerk at Cleveland, Ohio. A certified copy of one affidavit in the Lloyd Papers and the reproduction of other documents by Ida Tarbell make possible verification of this chapter (VII). These and extracts from an affidavit and a letter by John D. Rockefeller quoted in *Wealth against Commonwealth* make it apparent that, once the widowed proprietor of the Backus Oil Company had been induced to sell out, she was shown rather large consideration. Lloyd's sympathies had led him to accept uncritically the ex parte statements of Mrs. Backus. He was off guard, too, when he accepted without careful checking the exaggerated rumors in the Oil Regions that told of numerous suicides, bank failures, cases of insanity, and defalcations that resulted, supposedly, from the speculative frenzy that accompanied the rise of the oil monopoly.

In striking contrast with these lapses from accuracy are four chapters (XVIII–XXI) in *Wealth against Commonwealth* that describe the famous Buffalo criminal conspiracy trial of May, 1887. In it three trustees of the Standard Oil Trust and the president and vice-president of the Vacuum Oil Company of New York were charged with having conspired to blow up the works of a competitor and to injure its business in other ways. Lloyd's description of it is termed "one of the most dishonest pieces of so-called history he has ever read" by Professor Nevins, whose own account is based upon the incomplete transcript of testimony supplied to the House Committee of Manufacturers in 1888 by S. C. T. Dodd, chief counsel for the Standard Oil. Lloyd used the complete manuscript court stenographer's report, the Dodd transcript, the record of several pertinent civil suits, the contemporary press, interviews with the public prosecutors and complainant, and data derived from the then secret Trust Agreement and By-Laws of the oil monopoly. His account presents, therefore, not only the evidence offered in the conspiracy trial but also all knowledge pertinent to the issues involved. It is, in consequence, the fullest description of the case extant. On three separate occasions this lengthy narrative has been checked carefully and minutely against the court records at Buffalo of the criminal case and against the surviving records of the civil suits of the Buffalo Lubricating Oil Company against the Standard Oil and its subsidiaries. It has been compared also with the contemporary Buffalo newspapers, other periodicals, and with pertinent contemporary correspondence. The result of this process has been the verification of Lloyd's treatment almost line for line, even to the extent of establishing a moral certainty that one or two of the Standard Oil trustees on trial were involved in at least one aspect of the conspiracy, if not others, through voluntary adoption of its benefits. As for the president and vice-president of the Vacuum Oil Company, a three quarters owned Standard Oil subsidiary, there can be no doubt that they were convicted primarily for conspiring to blow up the works of the Buffalo Lubricating Oil Company, as Lloyd contends.

Nevins' description of the case for the defense (II, 80–86) would be more convincing *if* he had not omitted the damaging admissions made by defense witnesses under cross examination again and again; *if* the defense had not resorted almost entirely to mudslinging tactics in the trial and refused to put either the Everests or the Trustees on the stand; *if* the charge of Judge Haight to the trial jury had not emphatically stated that the question of the conspiracy to blow up the refinery of the Buffalo Lubricating Oil Company was *the central and most important issue* of the case; *if* the jury had not rendered a general verdict of guilty on all counts against the Everests to which each juryman adhered when polled at the request of the defense attorneys as soon as the verdict was returned; *if* the appeal by the Everests from this verdict to the higher courts had not omitted all mention of the count in the indictment that they had conspired to blow up their competitors' works as would surely have been done if the evidence on this, the most important part of the case, had been defective (*Appeal Book,* pp. 14–15); *if* as soon as the trial was concluded attempts had not been made to prepare the public mind for statements from the grand jury to the effect that the three trustees had never been properly indicted, which would undoubtedly have resulted in the production of affidavits from some of the grand jurors if the falsity of the charge had not been promptly exposed by a judge of the Supreme Court (Buffalo *Express,* May 19, 21, 1887); *if* this did not give added support to the assertion of District Attorney Quinby that the affidavits from six trial jurors, presented to Judge Haight prior to the sentencing of the Everests, by the latter's lawyers, had been secured with money (Tarbell, II, 106; Lloyd, p. 286); *if* Judge Haight in imposing a fine instead of imprisonment on the Everests had not given as the decisive reason for this action the fact that the convicted Everests were also being sued civilly for large punitive damages by reason of the same overt acts that had convicted them in the criminal suit, and that it was the duty of the criminal court under the rules of law to impose in the circumstances only a nominal penalty and thus prevent punishment for the same offense (MS. Opinion, "Hon. Albert Haight, Justice, The People, &c. vs. Hiram B. Everest and Charles M. Everest, May 8, 1888." Erie County Clerk's Office, *Proceedings and Actions*); *if* the district attorney just before the imposition of sentence on the Everests had not reminded Judge Haight that the act under which conviction had been secured contemplated the destruction of the works and business of a rival company (Buffalo *Express,* May 7, 1888).

Lloyd, rather than Nevins, follows the evidence that won the case. Lloyd (pp. 279–84) exposes thoroughly the collapse

of the case of the defense in the trial and the tampering by defense attorneys with witnesses which the prosecuting attorney had first exposed before the jury by forcing admissions under cross examination from the witnesses concerned. The charge of blackmail raised against Matthews by the defense during the trial and now by Nevins was fully considered by the jury. It was never proved, and if it had been, was irrelevant to say the least. This accusation was raised again and again by the Standard Oil and its defenders against competitors who defeated them in the courts, notably against Scofield, Shurmer and Teagle, and George Rice, charges that are repeated in Nevins' biography.

Charles B. Matthews to Lloyd, Oct. 12, 1886, Lloyd Papers (Winnetka), states that the district attorney, after just securing the indictment upon which the Everests and Standard Oil trustees were to be tried, had stated to him that the oral testimony taken by the grand jury, together with the affidavits and other documents then on file, were ample to convict all five defendants. This would seem to dispose of Nevins' charge (II, 84) that Matthews had induced the prosecuting attorney to indict the three trustees "without a shred of evidence that would bear examination in court."

So far as other specific charges by Nevins against Lloyd's account of the trial are concerned it may be stated: that although Albert A. Miller's character was completely destroyed before he testified in the criminal suit, his testimony was hardly as worthless as charged. Otherwise, the Vacuum Oil officials, with apparent knowledge and consent of 26 Broadway, would hardly have secreted him in Boston and then for several years in California, and attempted finally to get him out of the country. Miller's testimony, incidentally, stood up well under cross examination, and he adhered to the same story before both grand and trial juries. Lloyd in the light of the evidence given by attorney George Truesdale of Rochester, N. Y., the key witness for the prosecution, was fully justified in saying that the Everests had "coolly debated with lawyers the policy of blowing up a competitor's works" (pp. 248–49, although "a lawyer" instead of "lawyers" would have been more exact (*Bill of Exceptions*, pp. 197–99). The Everests though technically president and vice-present of the Vacuum Oil Company were in reality "employees of the trust" as Lloyd said, since the evidence presented in the trial showed that they simply executed orders from 26 Broadway, where seventy-five per cent of the stock in the Vacuum Oil Company was held by the Standard Oil Trust. Lloyd, on page 252, was referring undoubtedly to the "explosion" that blew off the safety valve of the overheated still since on pages 250–51 he had described carefully how the larger explosion intended to destroy the works of the Buffalo Lubricating Oil Company had failed to occur (compare Nevins, II, 336, n. 11).

If further comment were necessary it might be observed that if C. B. Matthews had abandoned his civil suit for $250,000 damages and had concentrated on the criminal action, the case for the people in the latter would have been considerably strengthened and might have led to the conviction of one or more trustees since under the rules of law the judge had to exclude from the criminal case some evidence of importance secured in the civil suits. This, in any case, would probably have resulted in a prison sentence for the Everests, since the judge ruled as he did in imposing fines instead. Adelbert Moot to C. B. Matthews, Apr.

20, 1893, Lloyd Papers (Winnetka), contains a considered condemnation by a competent attorney of Judge Haight's action in the trial in directing the jury to render a verdict of not guilty against the three trustees. Ida M. Tarbell's account of how H. H. Rogers tried to win her without avail to the Standard Oil interpretation of the case is well told in "Would Miss Tarbell see Mr. Rogers?" *Harpers*, CLXXVIII (Jan. 1939), pp. 142–44, and also in her autobiography.

The only other section of *Wealth against Commonwealth* under attack is that which (chapter XXVII) criticizes the United States Senate for refusing to investigate the election of Henry B. Payne. This passage is a carefully documented summary of the reasons offered by the state of Ohio to justify an investigation on the ground that the election had been secured corruptly by officials of the Standard Oil, and of the action taken by the Senate. As such it has stood up extremely well under careful checking against the sources, with one exception. Lloyd's contention that the Senate Committee on Privileges and Elections erred in reporting against an investigation would have been strengthened had he analyzed also the reasons given by the Republican senators Logan, Teller, and Evarts for opposing the investigation instead of ignoring them and leaving himself open to the charge of having deliberately suppressed the fact of their opposition in order to make his case. However, Lloyd used and cited Albert H. Walker's careful analysis of the entire question, which exploded the arguments and exposed the presumed motives of the three senators in question, and felt, no doubt, that it would be pointless to waste space on this aspect of the question. That Payne did not himself ask for an investigation by the Senate but actually opposed it, that the Standard Oil men charged with securing his election corruptly had kept out of Ohio during that State's limited investigation, that Ohio legislators more than sufficient in number to have decided the election were seriously implicated by evidence offered in support of Ohio's request for an investigation, together with evidence of continued Standard Oil control of the legislature that had elected Payne and the expressed convictions of informed leaders of both political parties in Ohio that the election had been corruptly secured by the Standard Oil was more than sufficient to justify the treatment contained in *Wealth against Commonwealth*.

Save for the exceptions noted, the accuracy of *Wealth against Commonwealth's* factual basis may be regarded as beyond dispute. Lloyd's deductions from the facts that he presented and the degree to which they were accepted by competent, contemporary scholars must now be examined. He was led at times into errors of judgment owing to the unavailability of inside information on the policies, organization, and economies of the Standard Oil. This accounts for the excessive emphasis that he placed upon railroad rate favors and the piratical methods employed by it and its imitators as sources of the economic power and wealth of the great combinations and their founders. It explains, partially, his statement that the oil monopoly had contributed little or nothing to the technology of the petroleum industry and his charge that it was actually opposed to technical improvements. Yet, with the possible exception of the Frasch process of purifying the Lima oils he was correct in stating that the basic processes and devices in use in the industry in 1894 came from pioneers and inventors outside of the combination. On the other hand Lloyd's own investigation established his contention that "the smokeless rebate," or railroad rate and service discriminations, was the chief weapon employed in the creation of industrial monopoly in late nineteenth century America. This conclusion was accepted by economists of the historical and welfare schools, such as John A. Hobson and Richard T. Ely, who were not bewitched by the evolutionary hypothesis. It received full corroboration, in the case of the Standard Oil, from the Commissioner of Corporations in 1906, and more recently from the account in Nevins' *Rockefeller*.

Lloyd's description of the evolution of monopolistic combination from the "corner," through the pool, trust, and holding company to the merger, and of the extension of its sphere of action from the national to the international field, has been accepted by virtually all students. His assertion that this development by 1893 had resulted in the monopolization or attempts to monopolize most necessities of life in America has been cited in Ida Tarbell's more recent survey. His analysis of monopoly price practices, made with the assistance of Byron W. Holt and E. Benjamin Andrews, discovered not only the greater rigidity of monopoly over competitive prices during periods of depression but it led him to assert that little if any of the reduction in costs that had characterized the oil industry since 1882 had been passed on to consumers by the Standard Oil save during sporadic periods of competition. These conclusions have been confirmed by subsequent investigations. John A. Hobson's contemporary but independent researches confirmed Lloyd's deduction that the oil trust's monopoly price policy entailed curtailment of production below the competitive level. That exorbitant profits were reaped by the Standard Oil from such a price policy is a conclusion in which Lloyd has the support of Allan Nevins. The further deduction that the great American fortunes of his day came chiefly from monopoly was confirmed by a contemporary study published by John R. Commons. The graphic description of the farflung investments and gigantic economic power of the Standard Oil group of millionaires, although admittedly incomplete, has been confirmed by such an investigator as Harold Faulkner. Lloyd concluded, as did Thorstein Veblen a few years later, that American capitalism, so dominated and conducted as described in *Wealth against Commonwealth,* was still in the hawk stage, predatory and speculative.

While presenting an almost impregnable array of facts and the most penetrating analysis of monopoly capitalism yet made in America, Lloyd launched a devastating attack upon its philosophical and ethical foundations. He was convinced that the monopoly movement was receiving great impetus from the extreme individualism and materialism of the age. He advocated, therefore, no return to free competition nor simple trust busting to cope with what he termed the "greatest social, political, and moral fact" of his day. The great combinations, he declared, had been sired by competition. Orthodox economics, with its reliance on individual self-interest as a guarantee of social welfare, had proved to be nothing but "a temporary formula for a passing problem." Monopoly was merely competitive business "at the end of its journey," rewarding the "fittest" with the power of life and death over the necessities of life, to be wielded by the same "self-interest" that had wrested this power from the public.

Lloyd knew, also, that for many a pragmatic American the business "'success" of the Standard Oil had demonstrated the economic soundness of large scale organization. He saw, too, that the "gospel of wealth," whose ostentatious piety and ever more widely advertised philanthropies Rockefeller practiced, cast a halo of sanctity about all that the oil monopoly did. Furthermore, it was clear that the official apology presented for Standard Oil by John D. Archbold and S. C. T. Dodd appealed to an urban reading public that was bewitched by the stereotypes of Social Darwinism. By reason of some uncanny insight Lloyd inferred, apparently, that Rockefeller himself secretly invoked the evolutionary philosophy of Herbert Spencer to justify his great raids upon the free enterprise system, just as he seemed to find in the doctrine of stewardship divine sanction for his swollen fortune. Careful reading makes it clear that the pitiless exposure in *Wealth against Commonwealth* of the cruel and illicit methods employed by the oil monopolists was motivated by a desire to strike down all the philosophical supports that the "Captains of Industry" relied upon to secure popular acceptance of the corporate business system. This is indicated by scores of allusions and illustrations in the book which Lloyd utilized to point up the grim contrast between the policies of monopoly and the philosophy and claims to public service professed by its adherents, between the religious philanthropies and prayer meeting attendance of the oil magnates and the Sabbath-breaking violation of the law by their natural gas subsidiary at Fostoria, Ohio. In this manner Lloyd sought to destroy the popular belief that the trusts were the product of an evolutionary process in the true sense, that

they or their wealthy managers represented the "survival of the fittest," or that
their great wealth was the reward for
either superior efficiency or greater moral
worth. Thus in pillorying Rockefeller
and the Standard Oil, *Wealth against
Commonwealth* exposed the falsity of
the "Gospel of Wealth of the Gilded Age,"
and the social evil wrought by application of Darwinian principles to business.
It demonstrated, also, how between the
greatest oil magnate and Henry Demarest
Lloyd the difference at bottom lay in the
philosophy with which each confronted
the problems of a business civilization.

Finally, Lloyd declared that the trust
movement was developing in direct an-
tagonism to the democratic heritage of
America. The combination movement, he
asserted, was destroying liberty. While
it was closing one economic province
after another to all but the privileged

few, it was subject to the law that gov-
erned tyranny everywhere as it reached
out to control the bench, manipulate
legislatures, shackle the press, and per-
vert pulpit and classroom to its own purposes. Under this impulse America was
moving toward an authoritarian system
that recognized no moral standards and
was evolving through industrial feudal-
ism toward the rule of a single, "corporate Caesar." By elevating "barbarians
from below . . . into seats of power kings
do not know" in America and Europe
monopoly capitalism was destroying
civilization itself as the process of perfecting the race through promoting human welfare in an atmosphere of liberty.
Thus, whether judged by its methods, or
ultimate consequences, or in the light of
its philosophical defenses, the trust movement was a veritable Frankenstein. . . .

Allan Nevins: LETTER TO THE EDITOR OF THE AMERICAN HISTORICAL REVIEW

To the Editor of the American Historical Review:

An unintentional disservice is sometimes done an able man by placing his title to remembrance upon grounds which, though perhaps related to the true basis of his distinction, are in themselves untenable. In my opinion Dr. Chester M. Destler has done Henry Demarest Lloyd precisely this disservice in his recent paper on that writer in the *American Historical Review* (October, 1944). He treats Lloyd as a sober, judicious, and absolutely veracious historian of American industry. In doing so he challenges a thesis which I presented as a minor element in my recent two-volume work on John D. Rockefeller: the thesis that Lloyd was an efficient and in some respects useful propagandist, but a signally untrustworthy historian. To this challenge an answer is required. While a thorough examination of the many inaccuracies, partisan misrepresentations, and other deficiencies of Lloyd's *Wealth against Commonwealth* would occupy an inordinate amount of space, I wish to offer some proofs of Lloyd's weaknesses, with special attention to those points at which Mr. Destler criticizes my examination of the book. That Lloyd was too biased, too limited of view, too abusive,

too prone to suppress facts adverse to his side of controversial cases, and too blundering in economic fields to make a dependable historian would be questioned by few who have read him in the light of an expert knowledge of our economic record; but general readers may perhaps desire a demonstration.

Mr. Destler begins with the vaunting remark that Lloyd had a "more penetrating mind" than Lord Bryce. Fortunately, this need not be taken seriously. The world has long since determined to measure the gifts of the author of *The Holy Roman Empire, The American Commonwealth,* and *Modern Democracies* by a much ampler measure than that supplied by H. D. Lloyd. More important is Mr. Destler's assertion that Lloyd was vastly superior to the so-called muckrakers, for Lloyd treated fully and cited exactly, while "the pat phrases of later writers rattled off the armor of great corporations." This is at variance with the facts. Lloyd's book was followed within the decade by a much superior work of the so-called muckraking school, Ida M. Tarbell's *History of the Standard Oil Company.* Miss Tarbell's volumes have been severely criticized, but as industrial history they are incomparably more thorough, shrewd, and careful than Lloyd's

Reprinted from the *American Historical Review*, 50 (April, 1945), 676–689, by permission of the editors and the author. The original article amplifies the argument in footnotes, here omitted.

book. Indeed, anybody who compares Tarbell and Lloyd will have one good measure of the latter's shortcomings. Mr. Destler further writes that the attack upon Lloyd comes in cycles and "is sharpest when, as in recent years, the papers of some of the capitalists of an earlier day" (he notes the "Standard Oil coterie" as especially hostile) are opened to historians. What papers? What capitalists? No Standard Oil papers save those of Rockefeller and J. N. Camden have been thrown open, and Camden's biographer ignores Lloyd. The attack on Lloyd's ideas is sharpest when some qualified economist deals with him; witness Gilbert H. Montague's work on the Standard Oil (1903), begun when Montague was Ricardo Scholar at Harvard.

In attempting to produce the impression that most criticism of Lloyd is of recent and dubious origin, Mr. Destler has to reckon with other writers than Tarbell, Montague, John T. Flynn, and myself — for by implication and comparison the first three expose Lloyd's faults nearly as much as I do. He has to reckon with the New York *Nation*, which when Lloyd's book appeared was the leading critical organ of the country, invariably expert, judicious, and responsible. Its literary columns were conducted without fear or favor by Wendell Phillips Garrison. The review of *Wealth against Commonwealth* was scathingly condemnatory. "This book," it began, "is a notable example of the rhetorical blunder of overstatement." A temperate, judicial presentation of evidence against the Standard Oil would have been useful. "But instead of this, we have over five hundred pages of the wildest rant. Much learning in the Standard Oil Company has made Mr. Lloyd mad. He raves more coherently at some times than at others;

but he is never perfectly sane." The *Nation* continued:

If we examine the particulars of the case presented by Mr. Lloyd, we find a number of them to be supported by questionable evidence. It is in the first place a very suspicious circumstance that Mr. Lloyd never mentions the names of the individuals whose conduct he denounces. . . . In the second place, Mr. Lloyd calls witnesses without discrimination. Some of them testify that they were bribed to commit arson and other crimes by the mysterious leaders of the Standard Oil Company. A dog would not be hung upon such evidence. Nor can Mr. Lloyd's citations of the evidence of reputable witnesses be allowed much weight, for he is so bitter in his advocacy that it would be grossly unfair to pass judgment upon his ex parte statement. It would be like deciding a case only after hearing the address to the jury of the plaintiff's attorney.

Upon the whole, Mr. Lloyd's book is abundantly calculated to arouse incredulity in the mind of any reader who understands the nature of evidence. . . . He appears to us to exhibit in his writings such indifference to truth, such incoherency of thought, such intemperance of speech, and such violence of passion, as to make him an undesirable leader. If reform can be had only through such reformers, it is better to endure our present ills. As to the Standard Oil Company, its history remains to be written, and the economic situation which it indicates remains to be described.

Now for a specification of flaws. It is clear, to begin with, that Lloyd never understood or tried to understand Rockefeller and his associates. In his article "The Story of a Great Monopoly" he wrote that "Rockefeller had been a bookkeeper in some interior town in Ohio, and had afterward made a few thousand dollars by keeping a flour store in Cleveland." Passing over the snobbery of this sentence (Lloyd achieved enjoyment of a handsome fortune by the easier method of marrying it), we find in its three blunders — Rockefeller was never bookkeeper in interior Ohio, never kept a flour store, and made much more than a few thousands in his commission business — proof of an indisposition to learn the truth about the oil magnate. Nowhere in *Wealth against Commonwealth* does Lloyd indicate any real effort to ascertain what manner of men Rockefeller, Rogers, Flagler, and Harkness were, why they had undertaken to organize the disorderly oil industry, and how they viewed their own aims. His unpublished letters are full of epithets like "robbery," "theft," and "depredation." Writing of "the essentially criminal character of what was done," he stated that the Standard heads "ought to be in the penitentiary." Without supporting facts, he accused them of employing a "condottieri." He wrote George Rice that the Standard men had been guilty of "piracies, treasons, and murders" — again without facts, for none existed. Such loose talk of treason and murder is not employed by responsible historians.

In *Wealth against Commonwealth* Lloyd wrote that Rockefeller and his partners had "dazzled the world by the meteor-like flash of their flight from poverty into a larger share of 'property' — the property of others — than any other group of millionaires had assimilated in an equal period." Here again we meet with blunders. The rise of the Standard Oil men to great wealth was not from poverty. It was not meteor-like, but accomplished over a quarter of a century by courageous venturing in a field so risky that most large capitalists avoided it, by arduous labors, and by more sagacious and farsighted planning than had

been applied to any other American industry. The oil fortunes of 1894 were not larger than steel fortunes, banking fortunes, and railroad fortunes made in similar periods. But it is the assertion that the Standard magnates gained their wealth by appropriating "the property of others" that most challenges our attention. We have abundant evidence that Rockefeller's consistent policy was to offer fair terms to competitors and to buy them out, for cash, stock, or both, at fair appraisals; we have the statement of one impartial historian that Rockefeller was decidedly "more humane toward competitors" than Carnegie; we have the conclusion of another that his wealth was "the least tainted of all the great fortunes of his day." But even without such evidence, Lloyd's reckless assertion that the Standard property was all stolen clearly bears no relation to historic or economic truth. It is not in the spirit of such utterances that the work of any industrial captain, or the complex story of the construction of any of the huge industrial edifices, is to be understood.

Of Rockefeller's true character (one broad side of which — austere, hardworking, home-loving, religious, and even in days of small means highly philanthropic — must command regard), Lloyd knew nothing. It may be said that Rockefeller's private character was no concern of Lloyd's. But had he learned something about it, he would have spared himself an egregious error. At one point, even Mr. Destler remarks, Lloyd did Rockefeller "less than justice." Less than justice indeed! Lloyd in *Wealth against Commonwealth* charged, in essentials, that Rockefeller had tyrannously brought a poor Cleveland widow, Mrs. F. M. Backus, into his power; that by threats, cajolery, and trickery he broke her resistance; that he forced her to sell for $60,000 a business "worth nearly $400,-000"; and that after thus robbing a defenseless woman, toiling for her "fatherless children," he brutally refused to let her keep even an interest of $15,-000 "in the business into which she and her husband had built their lives." Rockefeller was characterized as "the great man of commerce, who passes the contribution box for widows' mites outside the church as well as within." Filling a complete chapter, the tale was garnished with Lloyd's peculiar rhetoric: words like "slavery," phrases like "the maw or the morgue," and even a closing reference to the way in which "Dives once begged for a drop of water," which was intended to suggest that Rockefeller would soon languish in Tophet. This widely circulated tale did Rockefeller immeasurable harm. He had just founded the University of Chicago; he was planning other benefactions; his house was filled with missionaries and social workers; he was the principal lay pillar of the Baptist church; he was constantly consulting with such men as Drs. William Rainey Harper, W. H. P. Faunce, and Jacob Gould Schurman. But what a hypocrite this robber of widows was!

It is unnecessary to go into the evidence which has completely disproved every part of this bit of "history," and shown that the Widow Backus was treated with exemplary generosity. This evidence Lloyd could easily have found. Nobody now defends his story. Mrs. Backus apparently died wealthy. If the reader of these lines were accused of tricking and browbeating a helpless widow, and robbing her of a large sum; if the allegation were sown broadcast in repeated editions of a famous book; if he knew that his traducer could quickly

have ascertained its falsity, he would probably feel as Mr. Rockefeller always felt about Lloyd — that he was a "misguided man."

It is clear, again, that Lloyd never seriously tried to understand, in any historical sense, the industrial situation out of which the trust movement grew, or the circumstances under which the Standard and many like combinations were organized. He treats the rise of the Standard Oil combination, embracing leaders of the refining industry in Cleveland, Pittsburgh, Philadelphia, the Oil Regions, New York, and Baltimore, as a conspiracy to create chaos in a flourishing, prosperous industry for the enrichment of a few predatory men. He begins by painting a paradisical picture of the oil industry in its early years. Readers of *Wealth against Commonwealth* will find, in pages 40–43 inclusive, a dazzling account of a Golden Age in northwestern Pennsylvania. But into this elysium a serpent was preparing to creep. In 1863 — Lloyd says 1862, but this is an error — Rockefeller entered refining in Cleveland. Then "as early as 1865 strange perturbations were felt, showing that some undiscovered body was pulling the others out of their regular orbit." Still the Golden Age continued. But before the panic of 1873 general distress began to make itself felt. Some oil combination was putting an end to the happy era of prosperity. "Out of this havoc and social disorder," Lloyd laments, "one little group of half a dozen men were rising to the power and wealth which have become the marvel of the world."

The facts, as every careful student knows, are not only far more complex than this simple view suggests but point in the opposite direction. It was the disorder which preceded and caused the industrial combination; not the combination which caused the disorder. This was true alike of the oil industry, railroad industry, sugar industry, and many others. It is an elementary fact of economic history that in the great business efflorescence after the Civil War many industries suffered heavily from excessive expansion, overproduction, and cutthroat competition. Railroad rate wars in the 1860's and 1870's almost bankrupted many roads and gave rise to eveners' agreements and pools which by 1887 were almost universal. Excessive competition in the salt industry, causing sickening losses, again resulted in pooling compacts. To stop a savage competition of overgrown units which led straight to the bankruptcy courts, whisky distillers resorted first to pools and then to a trust, while the same conditions in the sugar industry prompted Henry Havemeyer to introduce the same remedy. In no industry was competition fiercer or more damaging than in oil refining. Here occasional periods of prosperity held out a glittering lure; rising world demand and advancing gold values assisted the boom; less capital was required to set up one of the early refineries than to establish a jewelry store or livery stable. In the spring of 1865 the Oil Regions had about thirty, with more fast being added; that fall Pittsburgh had eighty; by the following autumn Cleveland had more than fifty. They sprang up in the East all the way from West Virginia to Portland, Maine. The production of crude oil was equally unrestrained. Market gluts, price slashing, and disaster followed. What Dr. Paul Giddens in *The Birth of the Oil Industry* calls the "years of depression" began in 1865–66 at the time of the great Pithole rush, with its heavy oil production, and continued with intervals

of partial recovery until the national depression of 1873.

The evidence of this widespread overexpansion, harsh competition, and ruthless price cutting, contained in files of commercial newspapers, annual reports of boards of trade in Pittsburgh, Cleveland, and other cities, and statistics of the Chamber of Commerce of the State of New York, is summarized in some fifty pages of my life of Rockefeller, with citations far too numerous to list. Overproduction of crude oil forced well owners to set up rings and later to attempt stop-drilling agreements, but nothing could restrain the frenzied rush to new sites. Overproduction of refined oil naturally followed. Area competed with area, for the Oil Regions, Pittsburgh, Philadelphia, and Cleveland all wished to establish supremacy; railroads serving the different areas stimulated this rivalry. The margin between the price of a gallon of crude oil and a gallon of refined oil sank from 19½ cents in 1865 to 7⁹⁄₁₀ cents in 1870; and it required four gallons of crude to make three gallons of refined. Failures became commonplace. Indeed, the records of bankruptcy cases and testimony of commercial editors show that at times the situation was appalling. Yet there is not one line in Lloyd's chapter on these years to show overproduction and overcompetition, among well owners and refiners alike, was a factor in the depression. Mr. Giddens enumerates half a dozen contributory elements: unbalance between production and consumption, taxation, adverse export conditions, transportation difficulties, banking troubles, and speculative rings. Not one of these is mentioned by Lloyd. Intent on making readers believe his theory of a disruptive plot, a conspiracy against prosperity, he traces the difficulties entirely to a refiners' combination which did not exist even in embryo until 1872, and did not operate effectively until after 1873!

As Mr. Destler questions my statement regarding Lloyd's Golden Age, one of several passages may be quoted. Of this period Lloyd writes:

There was a free market for the oil as it came out of the wells and the refineries, and free competition between buyers and sellers, producers and consumers, manufacturers and traders. Industries auxiliary to the main ones flourished. Everywhere the scene was of expanding prosperity, with, of course, the inevitable percentage of ill-luck and miscalculation; but with the balance, on the whole, of such happy growth as freedom and the bounty of nature have always yielded when in partnership. The valleys of Pennsylvania changed into busy towns and oil-fields. The highways were crowded, labor was well-employed at good wages, new industries were starting up on all sides, and everything betokened the permanent creation of a new prosperity for the whole community, like that which came to California and the world with the discovery of gold.

Lloyd goes on to say that in 1869 the business had sprung to a net product of "6,000,000 barrels of oil a year" (the true figures for 1869 are just over 4,800,000); that the Oil Regions had "provided the financial institutions needed" (actually they depended heavily on outside banks, while the three pioneer oil exchanges at Titusville, Oil City, and Franklin were not organized until 1871); and that they had "built up towns and cities, with schools, churches, lyceums, theatres, libraries, boards of trade" (also with saloons, gambling hells, and other appurtenances of a rough boom area, and with a marvelous litter of wreckage as boom cities like Pithole were abandoned). The true picture of fierce in-

dividualism and mingled boom-and-bust in oil production and refining alike Lloyd does not give, for it would spoil his picture of Rockefeller's plot-against-the-Pennsylvania-paradise. Actually the situation was such that by 1871 railroad presidents and responsible refiners (the Logans of Philadelphia, Frew and Lockhart of Pittsburgh, Rockefeller and Flagler of Cleveland) were looking desperately for a remedy.

In short, Lloyd confused cause and effect; for nothing can be plainer than that it was chaos which produced combination and not combination which produced chaos.

Lloyd's misstatement of this basic situation is emphasized by his vague, confused, and erroneous presentation of the South Improvement Company. Correct in treating this company as indefensible, he is misinformed on much else. He asserts that Rockefeller was the "principal member" of the South Improvement Company. On the contrary, Rockefeller, like Flagler, entered it unwillingly (he had a very different plan of his own), never fully believed in it, and was probably glad when it was abandoned. Neither his name nor Flagler's was on the original list of stockholders. Neither became an officer of the company. Lloyd correctly treats the company as the product of joint action by certain railroads and refiners, but the emphasis of his exposition (like the above remark concerning Rockefeller) gives the refiners the more important role. Here he is wrong. The scheme originated with the oil-carrying railroads; its chief backers were Peter H. Watson of the New York Central-Lake Shore system and Vice-President Thomas A. Scott of the Pennsylvania; and Watson became president. Its main objects were to unite the oil-carrying railroads in a pool for the division of traffic, to unite the refiners in an association to act as traffic eveners, and to tie the two elements together by agreements which would stop destructive price cutting on refined oil and raise freight rates on petroleum. Rockefeller, preferring what he called "our plan" of a more completely integrated union of refiners, was continuously skeptical of "Tom Scott's scheme."

The vital differences between the two plans are completely missed by Lloyd in his astonishing assertion that the Standard Oil was simply the South Improvement Company revived. He wished to attach to the Standard the odium of the earlier combination. He therefore wrote of "the oil trust into which the improvement company afterwards passed by transmigration. Any closer connection there could not be. One was the other." We may well rub our eyes at this. One was the other! In reality, the stillborn South Improvement Company was an *ad hoc* creation; the Standard Oil combination was a slow growth over a period of a half-dozen years. The South Improvement Company was a very loose association of refiners, bound together only by agreements with each other and the railroads; the Standard Oil trust became a complete unification of properties. The South Improvement Company proposed to force other refiners to join by a crushing system of secret freight rebates; the Standard Oil combination was built up by purchase and merger — sometimes with the aid of rebates, sometimes not. The South Improvement Company was united like a Siamese twin to a railroad pool; the Standard stood apart from any railroad combination, and early in its history fought perhaps the most titanic industrial battle of the century with the Pennsylvania Railroad. The two organi-

zations had few resemblances and the most radical differences. The statement that "one was the other" is nonsense.

Thus we might track Lloyd through chapter after chapter. In dealing with the Standard Oil rebates (which I condemn as warmly as he) he omits all mention of the facts that widespread rebating antedated the Standard and even the Civil War, and that independent refiners took rebates as eagerly as Standard men. He essays at great length to justify the attempt of a political-minded auditor-general of Pennsylvania to tax the Standard, an Ohio corporation, not merely upon its Pennsylvania properties but on its whole capital stock and dividends, an attempt which utterly broke down in the courts (pp. 166–81). His treatment of the "immediate shipment" controversy (pp. 104 ff.) is highly misleading. He gives seventeen pages, with much tear-wringing rhetoric (pp. 181–98), to a suit against one of the Standard's component companies which the judge closed with a six-cent verdict. His statistics on prices can easily be riddled. On page 403 he finds something terribly sinister in the fact that William C. Whitney, identified as an "associate" of Rockefeller, was managing Grover Cleveland's 1892 campaign; Whitney was never an associate of Rockefeller and never connected with the Standard. So far we might regard Lloyd as merely ignorant and partisan, his sincerity standing unquestioned. But unfortunately his book contains material which throws suspicion on his literary integrity. Mr. Destler tries to exculpate him from two of my charges, giving a distorted statement of each. The evidence may here be briefly restated.

To the Buffalo conspiracy case of 1887 Lloyd allots the disproportionate space of forty-five pages. Hiram B. and Charles Everest, organizers of the Vacuum Oil

Company of Rochester, and John D. Archbold, H. H. Rogers, and Ambrose McGregor, through whom the Standard had bought a three quarters interest in the works, were indicted for allegedly conspiring to blow up the plant and otherwise destroy the business of the rival Buffalo Lubricating Oil Company, Ltd. The trial attracted wide attention. It ended in a fine of $250 each for the Everests and the acquittal of the three others! These are the basic facts on which Lloyd built an amazingly ex parte recital.

Lloyd offers at great length, with detailed comment, the entire case of the prosecution (pp. 243 ff.). He expatiates upon the rugged virtues of the head of the Buffalo company, Charles B. Matthews, and his associates Miller and Wilson. He excoriates the Everests for their alleged machinations to ruin these competitors. In ten sensational pages he describes how an employee was induced to sabotage the Buffalo plant; how he weighted the safety valve of the oil-still furnace and packed it with plaster; how he ordered the fire stoked till the firebox grew cherry-red; and how the plant was saved only because the plaster broke and the valve opened. But for this, Lloyd indicates, the Buffalo plant would have exploded into "acres of fire"; its men would have been "literally roasted alive." The Everests committed other alleged crimes; they spread damaging reports about the Buffalo company, enticed workers away, and brought vexatious patent suits. But their foulest act was this attempt at a horrible explosion and general holocaust.

The reader of Lloyd's account is left in amazement that criminals so monstrous should have been let off with paltry fines of $250, while their accomplices were freed — until the reader, if

wary, suddenly realizes that Lloyd has completely suppressed the evidence for the defense. On the vital point of the "explosion" (Lloyd uses the word again and again, and actually speaks of "the Buffalo explosion" though his own record shows that no explosion whatever took place) not a shred of the defense is offered. Yet its story is highly significant. A plant-management expert of the Standard, a Princeton graduate of twenty years' experience in refining, testified that it was general usage to attach safety valves to fire stills; that it was economical to build extremely hot fires to heat the petroleum as fast as possible; that "there is no such thing as making too hot a fire for the first two hours"; and that safety valves frequently broke open. Other experts testified that packing plaster of Paris in safety valves was common practice; it prevented leakage of gases in the still, but instantly broke when the valve blew open. An independent refiner of Philadelphia, of obvious honesty, corroborated all this; the safety valve was sound usage, and the cherry-red fire "occurs at almost every distillation in my knowledge."

Not only did Lloyd suppress all this, but he suppressed also the fact that the principal witness to the alleged sabotage was a brother-in-law of Matthews. He suppressed the evidence that in establishing the Buffalo plant Matthews and his associates Miller and Wilson had acted unethically; they were former employees of the Vacuum Oil Company, and they took steps to copy the special Vacuum process, reproduce some of the Vacuum machinery, and carry off the list of Vacuum customers. Lloyd also suppressed Wilson's testimony that Matthews had said that he expected to get $100,000 or $150,000 by getting the Standard to buy him out, and Matthews' own uneasy admission on the witness stand that he had said "something of that sort" — *i.e.*, that he might be bought out for a large sum.

These suppressions amount to falsification of the record. When the defense story is told, and not until then, we can understand why the Everests were let off with the inconsequential penalty of a $250 fine, and the three more prominent defendants acquitted. Men guilty of trying to blow up a factory are not treated so lightly. When the defense story is told we can understand why it was that, to quote Lloyd (p. 286), six of the jurors "signed a statement that the prisoners were found guilty, not because they had conspired to blow up their rival's refinery, but because they had enticed away Albert [an employee]." One juror certainly signed an affidavit that he believed the whole panel did not intend, "in rendering said general verdict, to pronounce the defendants guilty of an attempt or conspiracy to blow up or burn the works of the Buffalo Lubricating Oil Company, Ltd.," but simply guilty of enticement of a worker. By suppressing the defense, Lloyd placed himself under the necessity of supplying wild explanations of the result. He writes that the judge was crooked; "he failed to remember to observe the law" (p. 278). The six jurors were probably crooked; the district attorney accused them of taking bribes (p. 286). Even the minister of Matthews' church was crooked; he asked Matthews to drop his office in the church, simply because a Standard agent in the city had been "very kind to our pastor" (pp. 294, 295). H. H. Rogers, John D. Archbold, and Ambrose McGregor contended that their own indictment had been an afterthought of the district attorney in an effort to exploit anticorporation prejudices. Judge Haight directed their ac-

quittal on the ground that they clearly knew nothing about the alleged enticement or sabotage. Lloyd includes none of the facts which led Ida M. Tarbell, after careful study of the papers, to declare that their connection with the case "had been so indirect" that their indictment was quite unjustified.

The Buffalo case was a sorry episode in American industrial history. Nearly all those concerned with it (John D. Rockefeller was not one) emerge badly. In my life of Rockefeller I sharply censure H. H. Rogers and the Standard attorney, S. C. T. Dodd, for several acts. While nobody can now determine the exact degree of guilt attaching to the Everests, they had certainly behaved with gross impropriety and probably with some criminality. But among the sorry figures in the case is Lloyd. The charge against him is not that he failed to delve deeply into the evidence. It is that his eagerness to blacken the Standard led him to suppress one entire side of it. His chapters are larded with the usual question-begging rhetoric. Typical page headings include "Crime Cheaper Than Competition," "The Victim Punished First," and "Hardly a Mouthful for the Trust." He makes the most of every crumb for the prosecution. But that there was a case for the defense, and a strong case, no reader would ever guess.

A similar instance of *suppressio veri* is afforded by Lloyd's treatment of the Payne election case. Whether Henry B. Payne of Cleveland, a prominent Douglas Democrat before the Civil War and a prominent Tilden Democrat after it, was a beneficiary of bribery in gaining his Senate seat no man can now say. The undisputed facts are that in 1884 the Ohio legislature met with a Democratic majority; that the Democratic caucus gave Payne forty-six votes, Durbin Ward seventeen, and George H. Pendleton fifteen for the Senate seat; that the legislature then elected Payne with practically all the Democratic votes; and that disappointed Democrats soon raised a cry of bribery. When a Republican house came into power in Ohio in 1886 it took up these charges, which involved several Standard Oil men, and ordered an investigation by a select committee; fifty-five or sixty witnesses were heard; the minority report declared that "absolutely nothing" had been found in any way compromising the accused legislators; and the majority report, while declaring that "the testimony developed nothing of an inculpating character concerning the members of the House named in the resolution of inquiry," stated that the circumstances warranted sending the testimony to the United States Senate "for such action as it may deem advisable." The evidence was referred to the Senate Committee on Privileges and Elections; this body, after scrutinizing it carefully, reported in July, 1886, against any further investigation; and the Senate by a vote of forty-four to seventeen dismissed the issue. Historians may well regret that a Senate inquiry was not ordered. But the dismissal was not on party grounds, for both the Senate committee and the Senate itself were Republican.

Lloyd was eager to make his readers believe that the Standard Oil had bought Payne his Senate seat. Nearly all the Standard heads were Republican, uninterested in Democratic affairs; the idea that a man of Payne's high probity could be controlled in the Standard's interest is hardly tenable; and Rockefeller, who was sometimes evasive but never mendacious, has explicitly denied that the Standard interfered in this matter. We may put to one side the now insoluble question whether bribery swayed the election. For our purposes the material issue is the use Lloyd made of the available evidence. It was of course not enough for him to suggest bribery of a general character; it had to be Standard Oil bribery. His account is marked by these extraordinary features:

1. Lloyd makes great use of the fact that the chief financial manager of the Payne campaign at Columbus was treasurer of the Standard Oil. *He completely suppresses the fact that this man was Payne's son, with a filial motive for wishing his father in the Senate,* and the additional fact that, being independently wealthy, he was quite able to finance his own campaign operations.

2. Lloyd fails to mention that whereas the legislature which elected Payne was Democratic, the legislature which two years later asked an investigation was Republican.

3. Lloyd's statement of the presentation of testimony to the Senate is less honest than Miss Tarbell's. She writes: "The testimony did not prove the charge of bribery, the Ohio legislature said." Nor does Lloyd mention that the minority of the house committee in Ohio declared that the evidence was completely empty.

4. Lloyd tries to suggest throughout that the Ohio legislature was unable to get at a great deal of evidence that the United States Senate could have found. The fact is that the Ohio investigation was most searching. The majority of the house committee reported: "Whenever our attention was called to anything which indicated the probable employment of improper means to gain support, we followed the clews presented. . . . Our inquiries were not confined to the technical rules of legal proof, but the committee availed itself of any source of in-

formation — admitted hearsay statements, and even the opinions of witnesses." The minority reported that the committee had "exercised the greatest liberality possible in the taking of testimony, which has extended the scope of its inquiry far beyond the limits that could be given the most liberal construction of the resolution." The investigative powers of the Senate were actually narrower than those of the Ohio authorities.

5. Lloyd states that of the evidence brought from Ohio to the Senate (which included new material specially prepared by two Republican congressmen of Ohio) "none of the matter was presented on mere hearsay or rumor." As I say in my biography, "His own statement then proves that practically all of it was so presented." Men were willing to say they had *heard* this or that of bribery, but of direct evidence there was a minimum.

6. Describing the adverse report of the Senate elections committee, Lloyd makes a statement intended to suggest that it acted on partisan grounds. He writes of "senators Pugh, Saulsbury, Vance, and Eustis [Democrats] voting against Hoar and Frye." He suppresses the fact that three Republicans of high standing, William M. Evarts, a former Secretary of State, Henry M. Teller, a former Secretary of the Interior, and John A. Logan, onetime major general commanding the Army of the Tennessee, voted alongside Pugh, Saulsbury, Vance, and Eustis.

7. Lloyd, unlike Miss Tarbell, fails to mention the emphatic vote, forty-four to seventeen, by which the Senate dismissed the matter.

The point at issue here is not the question whether bribery was or was not used. No positive assertion on that question is now possible. The point is that

Lloyd does not make a fair statement of the evidence pro and con. It may be added that he accuses Payne, without evidence, of dishonest subserviency to corporate influence in his vote on the Interstate Commerce Bill (p. 388). Again we meet the rhetorical flourishes: "Coal-Oil Legislators," "The Senate Votes to Be a Market," "The Presidency on the Bargain-Counter." When did the Senate vote to be a market? When was the Presidency put on the bargain counter? If this chapter is history, a better name for the productions of true historians must be found.

At this point we may end our detailed traversal of Lloyd's pages. In noting his weaknesses, I do not intend to suggest for a moment that the Standard Oil and other monopolies were not guilty of great abuses. The voracities that accompanied the Standard's rise to power and that marked its long domination of the oil business are described with great fullness, and with much more precision than Lloyd offered, in chapter after chapter of my life of Rockefeller: "The Conquest of Cleveland," "Rockefeller and the Producers," "Sweeping the Board," "He Should Keep Who Can," and a dozen others. Far from excusing the Standard's interference with government, in a chapter on "The Standard in Politics" I offer a detailed specification of them and present the only clear proof yet given that the Standard's agents *did* once bribe a legislature: the Pennsylvania legislature in connection with the Billingsley bill of 1887. My summation of Standard Oil practices at points goes beyond Lloyd's, for it takes full note of "a cruel use" of railroad rate discriminations of espionage, of local price slashing to destroy competitors, of excessive profits, and of other evils. But it also takes note of the complex economic conditions which made the trust movement inevitable, of the laissez faire individualism which dominated business ethics, and of the Standard's many constructive achievements.

Some larger considerations remain to be briefly indicated. Lloyd, whose grasp of economic realities was never firm, failed to comprehend the deeper meaning of the great sweep of business consolidation which took place during his generation. The fundamental postulates of *Wealth against Commonwealth* fit the early machine capitalism of the United States before 1870; they do not fit a system wherein the means and scale of production had enormously expanded, small businesses had in great part become uneconomic, and huge aggregations of plant and capital could in many instances best serve society. If there is a paragraph of Lloyd's book which shows a realization that the ravages of unbridled competition were frequently more terrible than the ravages of monopoly, careful reading fails to discover it; yet evidences of this fact (and of the wastefulness of much small business) lay all about him. In the field of business history moral strictures, however enticing, cannot be substituted for a scientific study of rigid economic causes and compulsions. Lloyd, failing to understand that the movement for industrial concentration was primarily a reaction against deep-seated evils and a response to irresistible economic forces (forces which in the last four years have conspicuously made big business still bigger), fails to do any justice to its beneficial side. His book contains nothing remotely comparable to Miss Tarbell's chapter on "The Legitimate Greatness of the Standard Oil Company" and shows no understanding of those truths which Charles R. Van Hise shortly afterwards stated so vigorously in his *Concentration and Control* (1912). Nor did Lloyd comprehend the true implications of the trust movement for the government. In his final chapters he condemns the very policy of government regulation of business which the nation has found indispensable, terming it "a dream" and a compromise with evil (p. 533).

Family piety has given Lloyd two volumes of eulogy; it is to be hoped his next biographer will not substitute "the foolish face of praise" for a strict appraisal. He was not a historian intent upon impartial truth and sensitive to the injunction, *audi alteram partem;* not an economist; not a clear-eyed analyst of current facts and trends. He was a truly remarkable propagandist. It is a disservice to Lloyd to view him as a historian. Many of his faults and errors fade away if he is treated as a publicist and crusader, laboring in what multitudes thought a great cause; but they condemn him utterly if he is treated as a historical writer.

Suggestions for Additional Reading

Some of the books represented by excerpts in the preceding pages should be read in their entirety for a complete and circumstantial account of Rockefeller. This is especially true of Rockefeller's *Random Reminiscences of Men and Events* and Nevins's *John D. Rockefeller*.

For a further account of the Standard Oil monopoly as a significant form of industrial enterprise, the following references will be found useful: Burton J. Hendrick, *The Age of Big Business* (Volume 39 in Chronicles of America series, New Haven, 1919), Chapter 2; John Moody, *The Masters of Capital* (Volume 12 in the same series), Chapter 4; Gilbert H. Montague, *The Rise and Progress of the Standard Oil Company* (New York, 1903). Of special interest are the documents dealing with the origins of Standard Oil published by Chester McA. Destler under the title "The Standard Oil, Child of the Erie Ring, 1868–1872, Six Contracts and a Letter," *Mississippi Valley Historical Review*, 33 (June, 1946), 89–114.

Accounts and evaluations of the circumstances which made the rise of big business possible are to be found in Thomas C. Cochran, *The Age of Enterprise* (New York, 1942), and Ida M. Tarbell, *The Nationalizing of Business, 1878–1898* (Volume 9 of *A History of American Life*, New York, 1936).

Critical appraisals of the leaders of business enterprise after the Civil War are provided in Henry Demarest Lloyd, *Lords of Industry* (New York, 1910), and Matthew Josephson, *The Robber Barons* (New York, 1934). A recent recapitulation is contained in Chester McA. Destler, "Entrepreneurial Leadership: The 'Robber Barons': A Trial Balance," *The Tasks of Economic History* (September, 1946), pp. 28–49. Further discussion by Destler of his disagreement with Nevins's appraisal of Lloyd is available in a mimeographed essay titled "A Commentary on the 'Communication' from Allan Nevins in the *American Historical Review*, April, 1945," which may be obtained from the author.

The following writings will be useful for those interested in the organization of the oil industry and its place in the American economy: Myron W. Watkins, *Oil: Stabilization or Conservation* (New York, 1937); Roy C. Cook, *Control of the Petroleum Industry by Major Oil Companies* (Temporary National Economic Committee, Investigation of Concentration of Economic Power, Monograph 39, Washington, United States Government Printing Office, 1941); and *Review and Criticism on Behalf of Standard Oil Company (New Jersey) and Sun Oil Company of Monograph No. 39, with Rejoinder by Monograph Author* (the same, 1941). An interesting pictorial view of early conditions in the oil industry is presented by Paul H. Giddens, *Early Days of Oil* (Princeton, 1948).

An especially good short account of the problem of rebates is William Z. Ripley, *Railroads, Rates and Regulation* (New York, 1912), Chapter 6.

Somewhat surprisingly in view of the extent to which business leaders have formed prevailing social values, no very substantial body of fictional writing has used the businessman as a central figure. Most of the portrayals are critical in tone, as in Henry James, *The American* (1877); William Dean Howells, *The Rise of Silas Lapham* (1885); Theodore Dreiser, *The Financier* (1912) and *The Titan* (1914); and Sinclair Lewis, *Babbitt* (1922). More sympathetic characterizations appear in Booth Tarkington, *The Plutocrat* (1927), and Sinclair Lewis, *Dodsworth* (1929). An especially interesting treatment is to be found in F. Scott Fitzgerald, *The Great Gatsby* (1925).

110000